Supplemental Poverty Measure: A Comparison of Geographic Adjustments with Regional Price Parities vs. Median Rents from the American Community Survey

March 2014

Supplemental Poverty Measure: A Comparison of Geographic Adjustments with Regional Price Parities vs. Median Rents from the American Community Survey

Trudi Renwick, Bettina Aten, Eric Figueroa and Troy Martin

Abstract

One of the innovations of the Supplemental Poverty Measure is to make adjustments in the official poverty threshold to account for geographic price level differences, particularly for differences in the cost of shelter as measured by rents. A more recent initiative is to estimate thresholds that include price differences for goods and services other than rents.

The focus in this paper is to compare two types of geographic adjustments: one based on the ACS median rent index (MRI), and one based on a recently published set of state and metropolitan regional price parities (RPPs). The RPPs are of two types: an all item index that includes a broad group of expenditure classes and another that is more narrowly focused on just food, clothing and rents.

The differences between the MRI and the all item RPPs are significant for most states, resulting in higher poverty rates for 15 states and lower rates for 26 states. When the narrower RPPs are used, poverty estimates are higher than the MRI poverty rates in 20 states, lower in 22 states and not statistically different in 9 states. In metropolitan areas, the overall RPPs lower the poverty rates when compared to the MRI, because differences in the combined price level of goods and services are generally not as large as differences in rents. When the RPPs are constrained to food, clothing and rents, the poverty rates in metropolitan areas are greater than the MRI poverty rates.

Key Words: Poverty, geographic adjustments, RPPs

Introduction

Drawing on the recommendations of the report of National Academy of Sciences (NAS) Panel on Poverty and Family Assistance (Citro 1995)[1], and the subsequent extensive research on poverty measurement (Short, Garner, Johnson and Doyle, 1999, Short 2001), an Interagency Technical Working Group (ITWG 2010)[2] made a series of suggestions to the Census Bureau and the Bureau of Labor Statistics (BLS) on how to develop a new Supplemental Poverty Measure. In 2011 and 2012, the Census Bureau issued the first Research Supplemental Poverty Measure reports with poverty estimates for 2009, 2010 and 2011.

---

[1] For a summary of these analyses and recommendations, *see* Renwick (2011).
[2] In 2009 the Office of Management and Budget's Chief Statistician formed the Interagency Technical Working Group (ITWG) on Developing a Supplemental Poverty Measure. That group included representatives from the U.S. Census Bureau, Bureau of Labor Statistics, Economics and Statistics Administration, Council of Economic Advisers, U.S. Department of Health and Human Services, and Office of Management and Budget.

The ITWG suggested that the poverty thresholds be adjusted for price differences across geographic areas using the best available data and statistical methodology. The estimates in the Census Bureau reports use American Community Survey (ACS) data to adjust the housing portion of the poverty thresholds for differences in housing costs. This geographic cost index uses median outlays of renters for rent and utilities for two-bedroom housing units, henceforth referred to as the median rent index (MRI). See (Bishaw 2009, Renwick 2009, Renwick and Bishaw 2013) for a comparison of the different data sources and indexes related to rent price levels.

One shortcoming of the MRI is that it does not account for geographic differences in the cost of other elements of the poverty threshold. Both the 1995 NAS report and the 2010 ITWG concluded that while adjustment of the entire market basket may be desirable, adequate data on price differences for other elements did not exist.

In 2011, a research forum sponsored by the University of Kentucky Center for Poverty Research (UKCPR), in conjunction with the Brookings Institution and U.S. Census Bureau made further suggestions on the geographic adjustments to the poverty threshold. These suggestions included the use of quality-adjusted rental price levels, differentiation by metropolitan areas within states and the inclusion of other components of the consumption bundle.[4]

Over the past few years, the Regional Price Branch of the Bureau of Economic Analysis (BEA) has developed regional price parities (RPPs) that combine data from the BLS Consumer Price Index program with Census Bureau multi-year rents. The RPPs provide estimates of price level differences across regions for various consumption expenditure classes, including rents, food, apparel, transportation, housing, education, recreation, medical, and other goods and services.

This paper will compare state and metropolitan area poverty rates using the MRI to the rates found using RPPs. We begin by discussing the way the MRIs and RPPs are calculated and a summary of their differences, followed by the effect on poverty rates of applying these indexes to various population subsets. We conclude with an analysis of other measures that are related to poverty thresholds and future areas for research.

---

[4] All papers presented at the forum as well as the summary recommendations from the forum can be found at http://www.ukcpr.org/Conferences.aspx

I. The ACS Median Rent Index (MRI)

The MRI is the ratio of the median gross rent of a two bedroom unit with complete kitchen and plumbing facilities in a specific metro area or state to the U.S. median gross rent of the same type of unit (see Renwick 2011). The MRI is applied to the national threshold values, as defined by the Consumer Expenditure survey (CE), in proportion to the national average shares of housing and utility expenditures from total expenditures. The result is a metro area and state specific threshold values. The equation below depicts these steps:

$$Threshold_{ijt} = [(HousingShare_t \times MRI_{ij}) + (1 - HousingShare_t)] \times Threshold_t$$

- i = state
- j=specific metro area, other metro or nonmetro area
- t= tenure: owner with mortgage, owner without a mortgage, renter
- MRI = Median Rent Index
- HousingShare = percent of threshold represented by housing and utility expenditures
- Threshold = national average dollar value for income below which households are considered in poverty

Both the "threshold" values and the "housing shares" vary by tenure status, e.g. homeowner with a mortgage, homeowner without a mortgage or renter.

To "standardize" the housing units, the SPM index uses only two bedroom units with complete kitchen and bathroom. The index is constructed using the median rents and is not normalized.

The ITWG suggested using a different index, or at least a different weight to the index, for the three different thresholds. For 2011, shelter and utilities made up 49.7 percent of the renter threshold, 50.7 percent of the threshold for owners with a mortgage and 40.1 percent of the threshold for owners without a mortgage.[6]

The ITWG suggested that the geographic index be developed for specific metropolitan areas rather than using an average index number for all metropolitan areas in a single state due to the wide variation in housing costs across metro areas in some states. While the internal CPS ASEC files identify the Metropolitan Statistical Area (MSA) for all households on the file, when the Census Bureau releases the public use version of the file, MSAs with populations less than 100,000 are not identified. In addition, there may be some metropolitan statistical areas that are not in sample for the CPS ASEC.

MSA codes for portions of MSAs with populations smaller than 100,000 that could be identified by combining two geographic indicators (e.g. state and MSA) are suppressed. For several New England states, the CPS ASEC public use data discloses New England City and

---

[6] (http://www.bls.gov/pir/spm/spm_shares_200511.xls)

Town Areas (NECTA) rather than MSAs. The index was developed with these same geographic limitations.

The index used for the research SPM groups metro areas that cannot be disclosed into one group in each state, "other metro".[7] The remaining geographies, including micropolitan statistical areas, are categorized as "nonmetro" for each state. When a MSA or NECTA crosses state line, the median gross rent for the entire MSA or NECTA is used to calculate a single index value for the MSA.[8]

II.   Regional Price Parities

Regional Price Parities (RPPs) are spatial price indexes that measure price level differences across regions (such as states or metropolitan areas) for a given time period. The RPPs are based on annual averages for rents in each area and five-year rolling average price levels for other categories of goods and services.[9]

The RPPs are constructed in two stages. The first stage uses price and expenditure inputs collected for the Bureau of Labor Statistics (BLS) Consumer Price Index (CPI) program and the BLS Consumer Expenditure Survey (CE). CPI price data are available for 38 urban areas, while CPI expenditure weights, derived from CE survey data, are available for the 38 urban areas plus four additional rural regions.

In the second stage, the price levels and expenditure weights are allocated from CPI areas to all counties in the United States[10,11]. They are then recombined for regions, such as states and metropolitan areas, for which final RPPs, including an all item RPP, are estimated. This stage incorporates data for housing from the Census Bureau's American Community Survey (ACS): rent price levels are estimated directly from the ACS: annually for states, and across 3 years for

---

[7] The "other metro" group also includes portions of identifiable MSAs which cannot be identified or are not in the CPS ASEC sample. For example, the Wisconsin portion of the Minneapolis-St. Paul-Bloomington, MN-WI MSA is not identified in the CPS ASEC public use data. Therefore, the Wisconsin households in the Minneapolis MSA in the ACS data will be grouped with Wisconsin's "Other Metro" areas. The housing costs for these "other metro" areas are used to create the index to adjust the thresholds for CPS ASEC households in the Wisconsin portion of the Minneapolis MSA.

[8] Currently, all definitions for geographic areas on these lists reflect the June 30, 2003 Office of Management and Budget's (OMB) definitions. These are updated every ten years on the CPS ASEC file.

[9] In 2013, BEA released annual RPPs for 2007 to 2011 (Aten, Figueroa and Martin, 2013). Previous releases contained RPPs covering 5-year periods (Aten, Figueroa and Martin, 2011 and 2012).

[10] For the allocation, each county is assumed to have the same price levels as the CPI sampling area in which the county is located. Price levels in rural counties in the South, Midwest and West regions are assumed to be the same as those in the BLS urban, nonmetropolitan area for the region. BLS has no urban, nonmetropolitan area for the Northeast so rural counties are assumed to have the same price levels as those in the BLS-defined small, metropolitan areas of the Northeast.

[11] Expenditure weights are allocated to counties in proportion to household income. The allocation uses county-level ACS Money Income for the 2007–2011 period. Census money income is defined as income received on a regular basis (exclusive of certain money receipts such as capital gains) before payments for personal income taxes, social security, union dues, Medicare deductions, etc. Therefore, money income does not reflect the fact that some families receive part of their income in the form of noncash benefits. For more information, see www.census.gov. In past papers, population was used to distribute the weights; for a comparison, see Figueroa, Aten, and Martin (forthcoming).

metropolitan areas.[12] The estimates are quality-adjusted using a hedonic model that controls for basic unit characteristics such as the type of structure, the number of bedrooms and total rooms, when the structure was built, whether it resides in an urban or rural location, and if utilities are included in the monthly rent. Additional research on rent estimates using the ACS and CPI Housing surveys is available in Martin, Aten, and Figueroa (2011).

The weights for the rent expenditure class are also replaced with estimates derived from the 5-year ACS file, broken down into several types of housing units: from one bedroom apartments to detached houses with three or more bedrooms.[13] In addition, shares for the 16 expenditure classes are adjusted to reflect the valuation in BEA's personal consumption expenditures (PCE), yielding weights consistent with BEA's national accounts.[14] This adjustment shifts the distribution of weights across expenditure classes, notably reducing the share of rents expenditures from total consumption in the United States from 29.5 percent to 20.6 percent.

The RPPs published by BEA represent metropolitan and nonmetropolitan portions of states, or individual MSAs (which may cross state boundaries), plus the nonmetropolitan portion of the US. In order to match one of the recommendations of the ITWG, the metropolitan portion of each state was broken down into its MSA components. The RPPs are reweighted so that the average of the individual MSAs within each state, plus the nonmetropolitan portions of each state, is 100, the national average price level.

Since the SPM thresholds include only specific portions of the overall consumption basket (food, clothing, shelter and utilities), the overall RPPs published by the BEA may not be the appropriate geographic cost adjustment mechanism. The prices for food, clothing, shelter and utilities may exhibit different geographic cost variations than the other goods in the consumption bundle. Therefore, this paper uses another set of RPPs that were estimated by BEA researchers for this analysis. This second set provide index values for three distinct items: food, clothing and shelter. These separate indexes are used to adjust the SPM thresholds using the weights provided by BLS for each component of the thresholds for each tenure type.

---

[12] In Aten and D'Souza (2008), the imputation for county-level owner-occupied rent levels used owner's monthly housing cost data from the 5-year ACS housing file, together with the annual CPI Housing Survey from BLS. In more current work (Aten, Figueroa, and Martin 2011, 2012b), only observed rent price levels from the ACS were used, making no imputations for the owner-occupied rent levels. The monthly housing costs in the ACS include mortgage payments, but do not specify the term or interest rate of the loan. The coverage and distribution of the reported payments was highly variable, and using that information has been postponed until more data or further research is completed.

[13] For more information on how the RPP program estimates expenditures on owner-occupied rents, see Aten, Figueroa, and Martin (2012a).

[14] The adjustment is based on BLS research providing PCE-valued weights for CPI item strata (Blair 2012).

The following formulas describe how the RPPs are used in this paper to adjust the SPM thresholds. For the overall RPP:

$$Threshold_{ijt} = RPP_{ij} \times Threshold_t$$

- i = state
- j = specific metro area, other metro or nonmetro area
- t = tenure: owner with mortgage, owner without a mortgage, renter
- RPP = Overall RPP
- Threshold = national average dollar value for income below which households are considered in poverty

The "threshold" values vary by tenure status, e.g. homeowner with a mortgage, homeowner without a mortgage or renter. Note that unlike the MRI, the same geographic adjustment factor is used for each tenure type.

For the item-specific RPP, the formula is

$$
Threshold_{ijt}
$$
$$
= \Big(HousingShare_t \times rent\_rpp_{ij} + FoodShare_t \times food_{rpp_{ij}}
$$
$$
+ ApparelShare_t \times app\_rpp_{ijt} + OtherShare_t \Big) \times Threshold_t
$$

- i = state
- j = specific metro area, other metro or nonmetro area
- t = tenure: owner with mortgage, owner without a mortgage, renter
- MRI = Median Rent Index
- HousingShare = percent of threshold represented by housing and utility expenditures
- FoodShare = percent of threshold represented by food purchases
- ApparelShare = percent of threshold represented by clothing purchases
- OtherShare = percent of threshold not food, clothing or housing
- Threshold = national average dollar value for income below which households are considered in poverty

Both the "threshold" values and the expenditure shares vary by tenure status, e.g. homeowner with a mortgage, homeowner without a mortgage or renter. The RPP for rent is used for both rent and utilities. No adjustment is made to the residual "other" component of the thresholds.

In the following section we show the RPPs and the ACS Median Rent index for all the states and component MSAs, followed by a discussion of their effect on the poverty rates for different population subsets.

III. Results[17]

The results are divided into a) the difference between the RPPs and the MRI and the resulting threshold values, and b) the difference in poverty rates when these threshold values are applied to the income reported in the CPS ASEC. Poverty rates for states are based on pooling three years of CPS ASEC data (2010, 2011, 2012). All other poverty estimates use the 2012 CPS ASEC which provides poverty estimates for calendar year 2011.

Thresholds

Table 1 provides the index values for the RPPs and the MRI for specific MSAs, nonmetro areas in each state and other metro areas in each state and applies these index values to the 2011 threshold for SPM resource units that are renters with two adults and two children.

The 2011 MRI thresholds for SPM resource units who were renters with two adults and two children ranged from $20,163 for nonmetro North Dakota to $34,310 for San Jose-Sunnyvale-Santa Clara CA MSA. For the overall RPP-adjusted thresholds, the values ranged from $20,334 for nonmetro South Dakota to $31,053 for the Honolulu, HI MSA. The item-specific RPP-adjusted thresholds ranged from $17,987 for nonmetro Arkansas to $38,359 for San Jose-Sunnyvale-Santa Clara CA MSA. The official threshold for SPM units of this size was $22,811 regardless of location. The difference between the highest and lowest threshold for the MRI was $14,147, the range for the overall RPP-adjusted thresholds was $10,719 while the range for the item specific RPP thresholds was $20,372.

National Poverty Rates

Table 2a displays 2011 poverty rates using the three indices for the nation as a whole as well as by selected characteristics. The national poverty rates for 2011 using the overall RPPs are lower than the national poverty rates using the MRI but the poverty rates using the item specific RPPS are higher than the poverty rates using the MRI. Using the MRI, the national poverty rate for 2011 was 16.1 percent while using the overall RPPs the national poverty rate was 15.6 percent. Using the item-specific RPPs the national poverty rate was 16.4 percent. Since the national poverty rates vary by the index used, it is useful to look beyond poverty rates for specific demographic groups to the distribution of the poor by demographic characteristics as shown in Table 2b.

---

[17] The estimates in this paper are from the 2009, 2011, and 2012 Annual Social and Economic Supplements (ASEC) to the Current Population Survey (CPS). The estimates in this paper (which may be shown in text, figures, and tables) are based on responses from a sample of the population and may differ from actual values because of sampling variability or other factors. As a result, apparent differences between the estimates for two or more groups may not be statistically significant. All comparative statements have undergone statistical testing and are significant at the 90 percent confidence level unless otherwise noted. Standard errors were calculated using replicate weights. Further information about the source and accuracy of the estimates is available at <www.census.gov/hhes/www/p60_243sa.pdf>.

Poverty Rates and Distribution of the Poor by Metropolitan Status

Using the overall RPPs to adjust the thresholds, decreases poverty rates using the MRI adjustment for those living outside metropolitan statistical areas and for those inside metropolitan statistical areas. The 2011 poverty rates for those outside MSAs decreases from 13.4 percent using the MRI to 13.2 percent using the overall RPPs. For those inside MSAs in principal cities, the poverty rate falls from 21.6 percent to 21.0 percent. For those inside MSAs but outside principal cities (suburbs) the poverty rate falls from 13.4 percent to 12.8 percent.

Using the item-specific RPPs increases poverty rates for those living in MSAs, inside and outside principal cities. The poverty rate for those outside metropolitan statistical areas falls from 13.4 percent using the MRI to 11.9 percent using the item-specific RPPs. The poverty rate for those living in principal cities increases from 21.6 percent using the MRI to 22.6 percent using the item specific RPP. The poverty rate for those living inside metropolitan statistical areas but outside principal cities increases from 13.4 percent to 13.8 percent.

As a consequence, there are shifts in the distribution of the poverty population. Table 2b shows the share of the overall population and the share of those in poverty using each index in each location. Using the overall RPPs, the share of the poor living outside MSAs increases from 12.8 percent to 13.0 percent. The change in the share of the poor living inside principal cities is not statistically significant while the share living inside MSAs but outside principal cities falls from 43.4 percent to 43.0 percent.

Using the item-specific RPPs, the share of the poor living outside metropolitan statistical areas falls from 12.8 percent to 11.1 percent while the share of the poor living inside metropolitan statistical areas increases.

Poverty Rates and Distribution of the Poor by Region

Using the RPPs to geographically adjust the thresholds instead of the MRI index results in statistically significant changes in poverty rates for all four regions. Using the overall RPP, poverty goes up in the Northeast from 15.0 percent to 15.5 percent. Poverty rates are lower for the Midwest (12.8 to 12.5), the West (20.0 to 18.8) and the South (16.0 to 15.3). *See* Table 2a.

Using the item-specific RPPs, the poverty rates go up in both the Northeast and the West but go down in the Midwest and the South relative to the MRI poverty rates..

The shares of the poor living in the West and the South fall when using the overall RPP compared to the MRI. In the West the share falls from 29.3 percent using the MRI to 28.4 using the overall RPPs. In the South the share falls from 37.1 percent to 36.7 percent. The shares of the other regions increase. The share of the Northeast increases from 16.6 percent to 17.7 percent while the share living in the Midwest increases from 17.0 percent to 17.2 percent. *See* Table 2b.

Using the item-specific RPPs, the shares of the poor living in the Midwest and the South fall while the shares of the poor living in the Northeast and the West increase.

Poverty Rates and Distribution of the Poor by Age

Using the overall RPPs to geographically adjust the thresholds reduces the poverty rate for each of the three major age categories. The poverty rate for children is reduced from 18.0 percent to 17.4 percent. The poverty rate for nonelderly adults is reduced from 15.5 percent to 15.0 percent. The poverty rate for those aged 65 and older falls from 15.1 to 14.7 percent.

Using the item-specific RPPs to adjust the thresholds increases the poverty rates for two of the three age groups, from 18.0 percent to 18.5 percent for children, from 15.5 percent to 15.8 percent for nonelderly adults. The change in the poverty rate for those aged 65 and older is not statistically significant. *See* Table 2a.

The changes in the distribution of the poor among the three age groups are not statistically significant for either version of the RPPs. *See* Table 2b.

State Poverty Rates

Table 3 displays poverty rates using the MRI and the RPP indices by state for 2009-2011 and compares each of these to a poverty rate calculated without geographic adjustments to the thresholds. The choice of cost of living adjustment mechanism influences the magnitude of the change in the poverty rate but not the direction. If statistically significant, the change between the unadjusted and the adjusted SPM poverty rate was in the same direction for all three cost of living adjustment options.[18]

For example, in California the unadjusted poverty rate is 16.8 percent. Using the MRI the poverty rate increases to 23.5 percent. Using the overall RPP index the poverty rate falls to 21.0 percent but using the item-specific RPP the poverty rate goes up to 26.9 percent. On the other hand, in West Virginia, the unadjusted poverty rate is 16.2 percent. Using the MRI to adjust the SPM thresholds the poverty rate falls to 12.3 percent. Using the overall RPP index the poverty rate increases to 12.6 percent. Using the item-specific RPP index the poverty rate falls to 11.0 percent.

Comparing the magnitude of the change between the unadjusted SPM Poverty rates and the poverty rates generated by each index:

- There are 18 states for which the difference between the MRI and the unadjusted SPM and the difference between the overall RPP and the unadjusted SPM are statistically significant. For 14 of these states, the MRI generates a larger adjustment than the overall RPP.
- There are 27 states for which the difference between the MRI and the unadjusted SPM and the difference between the item-specific RPP and the unadjusted SPM are

---

[18] For eight states, one or more of the index options results in a poverty rate that is not statistically different than the unadjusted poverty rates: Colorado (MRI); Illinois (MRI), Minnesota (MRI, Item Specific RPP), Oregon (Item Specific RPP), Pennsylvania (All Item RPP), Vermont (MRI, All Item RPP), Virginia (All Item RPP), and Washington (MRI). None of the three options results in a statistically different poverty rate for Arizona.

statistically significant. For 24 of these states, the item-specific RPP results in a larger adjustment than the MRI.

Table 4 and the following map display the differences between the poverty rates using the MRI and the overall RPP by state for 2009-2011. Using the overall RPPs to adjust the thresholds rather than the MRI results in statistically significant changes in the three-year average poverty rates for 41 states. The differences are not statistically significant for 9 states (Alabama, Arizona, Arkansas, Iowa, Oklahoma, South Dakota, Tennessee, Vermont, and Washington) and the District of Columbia.

Difference between SPM Poverty Rates: Overall RPP vs ACS Geographic Cost Adjustment: 2009-2011

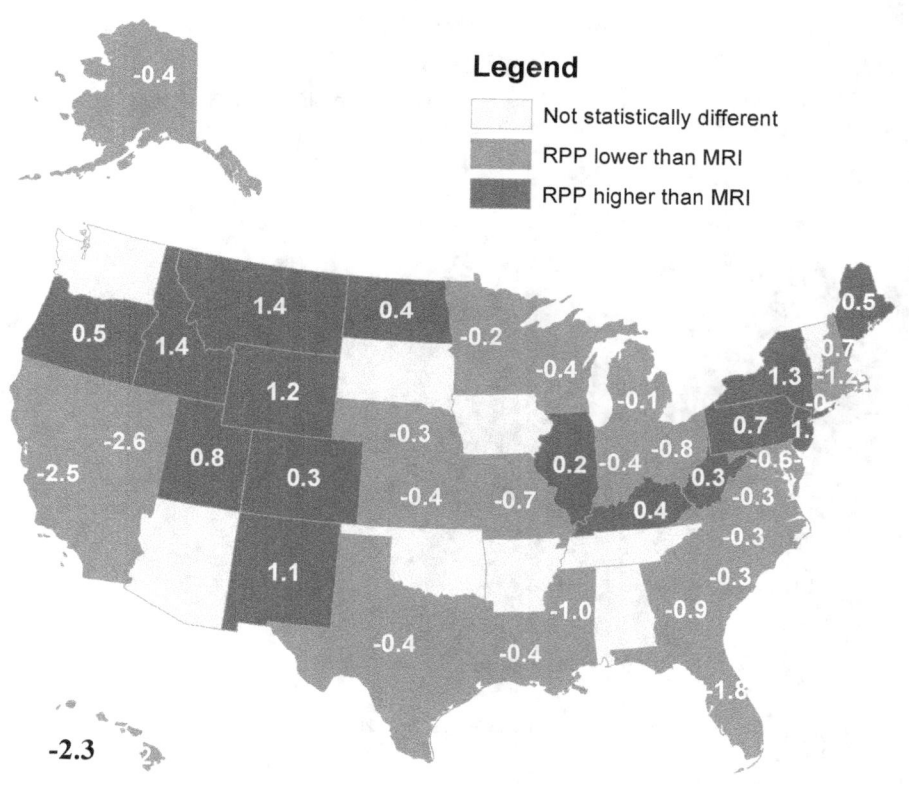

Source: Current Population Survey Annual Social and Economic Supplements 2010-1012.

For 15 states, using the overall RPP index results in higher poverty rates. The states with the largest percentage point increases are: Idaho, Montana , New York, New Jersey, Wyoming and New Mexico.[19] For 26 states, using the overall RPP index results in lower poverty rates. The four states with the largest percentage point reductions in their poverty rates are Nevada (2.6), California (2.5), Hawaii (2.3) and Florida (1.8).

---

[19] The increases for New Jersey was not statistically greater than the increase for Utah; the increases for Wyoming and New Mexico were not greater than the increases for Utah and Pennsylvania.

Using the item-specific RPPs, there are 41 states plus the District of Columbia with statistically significant changes in their poverty rates relative to the MRI poverty rates. The item-specific RPP poverty rates are higher than the MRI poverty rates in 19 states and the District of Columbia and lower in 22 states. There are nine states for which the differences are not statistically significant. The changes in the poverty rates range from an increase of 4.4 percentage points for the District of Columbia to a decrease of 2.2 percentage points for Mississippi.[20]

Difference between SPM Poverty Rates:
Item Specific RPP vs ACS Geographic Cost Adjustment: 2009-2011

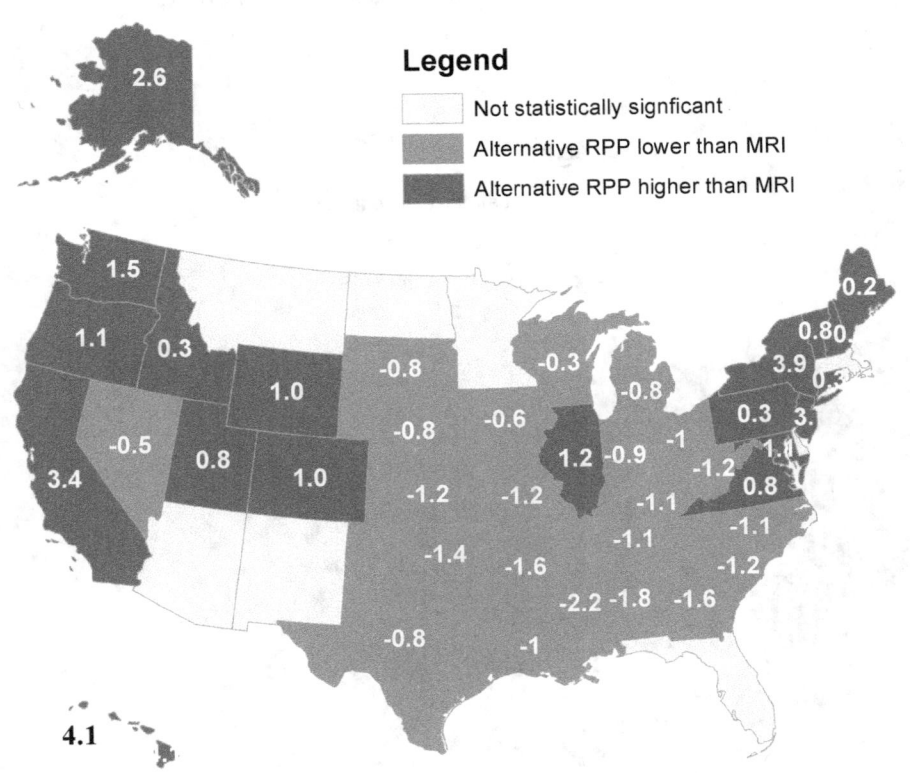

Source: Current Population Survey Annual Social and Economic Supplements 2010-1012.

V . Analysis

Relative to the poverty estimates using the MRI, the poverty rates using the overall RPPs are lower in some high costs states (e.g. California) but higher in other high cost states (e.g. New York). Likewise, the overall RPPs moderate the downward adjustments to the thresholds in some low cost states (e.g. Montana) but increase the downward adjustment in other low cost states (e.g. Georgia).

---

[20] The difference in the increases for the District of Columbia, Hawaii, New York and New Jersey were not statistically significant. The differences in the decreases for Mississippi, Alabama, Arkansas and Georgia were not statistically significant.

There are two major differences between the MRI index and the overall RPP difference. First, the RPP index covers all goods and services while the MRI represents only the differences in housing costs. Second, the MRI weights housing using the share of the SPM thresholds representing housing costs while the RPP weights housing consistent with its share of total consumption in the United States.[21]

In the MRI index, there is an implicit assumption that there are no differences in the cost of other goods and services in the SPM threshold. The overall RPPs offer a solution to this shortcoming by including a broad basket of goods and services. If the costs of other good and services vary directly with the cost of housing, the MRI adjustments will be too mild. On the other hand, if the costs of other goods and services vary inversely with housing costs, the MRI adjustments would be too strong.

However, the overall RPPs adjustment includes many goods and services that are not included in the SPM thresholds. If, for example, medical services are much more costly in one area, these differences should not be reflected in the SPM thresholds. In calculating the SPM, reported medical out of pocket expenses are subtracted from income before estimating poverty status. Therefore the differences in the cost of medical care will be reflected on the income side and should not be considered on the threshold side of the equation.

The differences between the poverty rates using the MRI and the poverty rates using the overall RPPs are largely driven by the different implicit weights given to shelter costs in the two approaches. The MRI poverty rates use the percent of the SPM threshold associated with shelter costs for each of the three tenure types. This ranges for 2011 from 50.7 percent of the threshold for owners with a mortgage to 40.1 percent for owners without a mortgage. The share for renters was 49.7 percent. On the other hand, the national average share of shelter costs in the overall RPP index is 20.6 percent for all tenure types.[22]

The differences in weights stem from the differences in the conceptual underpinnings of each index. The MRI is designed to measure differences in the cost of the items specifically included in the SPM thresholds – food, shelter, clothing, utilities plus a "little bit more". On the other hand, the weights in the RPP index are designed to be consistent with BEA's national accounts that cover a much broader range of goods and services than what is included in the SPM thresholds.

Using the item-specific RPP index enables us to make a more meaningful comparison to the MRI poverty rates. The item-specific RPP index uses the same weight for housing as the MRI index and provides a mechanism to examine the importance of adjusting for the differences in the cost of food and clothing as well as housing costs without including expenditure categories that are not included in the SPM thresholds. Comparing the differences between the item-specific RPP poverty rates and the MRI poverty rates relative to the SPM estimates without geographic adjustments, there were statistically significant differences in 26 states and the District of Columbia. There were only three states in which the MRI adjustments were stronger than the item-specific RPP adjustments.

VI. Further Research

In addition to the development of the RPPs discussed in this paper, there has been some other promising research on regional variation in the cost of other basic necessities. USDA has developed an index that uses Nielsen Homescan data to measures regional variation in food prices for 52 goods in 35

---

[21] In addition, the RPPs use a hedonic model to quality-adjust rent estimates while the MRI uses a simple median. The only quality adjustment in the MRI calculation is the exclusion of units lacking complete kitchens and plumbing. Previous research found that an index using the hedonic model was highly correlated with the MRI. *See* Renwick (July 2011, p. 10).

[22] Expenditure shares do vary across the 38 CPI sampling areas.

market groups (Todd, Mancino, Leibtag and Tripodo, 2010).[23] Carillo, Early and Olsen (2012) have developed a panel of price indices for housing, other goods, and all goods for each metropolitan area and the nonmetropolitan areas of each state from 1982 through 2010 using housing cost data from the 2000 HUD Customer Satisfaction Survey, data from 2000 Decennial Census and the price indices for non-housing goods produced each quarter for many urban areas by the Council for Community and Economic Research (formerly the American Chambers of Commerce Research Association or ACCRA). A recent Census Bureau working paper examines metro-level differences in commuting costs.[24]

Extensions of this research could include the production of a RPP index that treats utilities separately from rent and an investigation as to whether any of the RPP components would be the appropriate adjustment mechanism for the "other" category of the SPM thresholds. Another potential research area is the question of whether or not differences in amenities should be taken into account in making geographic adjustments to the thresholds, and if so, mechanisms for doing this.

In addition, state specific work on the Supplemental Poverty Measure continues to generate additional research questions. In creating the California Poverty Measure, researchers questioned the use of the same geographic adjustment factor for all three tenure groups. They argue that in California, while homeowners with a mortgage and renters have housing costs much higher than the national average, as a result of Proposition 13, homeowners without a mortgage face housing costs much closer to the national average. (Not because they do not have a mortgage per se but because they tend to have lived in the same home for a longer period of time and therefore have been protected from property tax increases by Proposition 13). The California Poverty Measure also makes an adjustment in commuting expenses to reflect the reduced expenditures of those who work at home or ride a bike to work.

---

[23] Renwick and Bishaw (2013) explored the impact of this index on SPM poverty rates. The poster can be found at http://www.census.gov/hhes/www/poverty/publications/PAA_Where_are_the_Poor_Do_prices_matter.pdf
[24] Edwards, et.al. (2014).

References

Aten, Bettina H. 2005. "Report on Interarea Price Levels." Bureau of Economic Analysis (BEA) Working Paper 2005–11; www.bea.gov/papers

Aten, Bettina H. 2006. "Interarea Price Levels: An Experimental Methodology." Monthly Labor Review 129 (September): 47–61; www.bls.gov.

Aten, Bettina, Eric Figueroa and Troy Martin. April 2011. "Notes on Estimating the Multi-year Regional Price Parities by 16 Expenditure Categories: 2005-2009." www.bea.gov/papers.

Aten, Bettina H., and Roger J. D'Souza. 2008. "Regional Price Parities: Comparing Price Level Differences Across Geographic Areas." SURVEY OF CURRENT BUSINESS 88 (November): 64–74; www.bea.gov.

Aten, Bettina H., Eric B. Figueroa, and Troy M. Martin. 2012b. "Regional Price Parities for States and Metropolitan Areas, 2006-2010." SURVEY OF CURRENT BUSINESS, 92 (August): 229-242; www.bea.gov.

Aten, Bettina H., and Marshall B. Reinsdorf. 2010. "Comparing the Consistency of Price Parities for Regions of the United States in an Economic Approach Framework." Paper presented at the 31st General Conference of the International Association for Research in Income and Wealth in St. Gallen, Switzerland, August 27; www.bea.gov/papers.

Bohn, Sarah, Caroline Danielson, Matt Levin, Marybeth Mattingly and Christoper Wimer. 2013. The California Poverty Measure: A New Look at the Social Safety Net. Public Policy Institute of California. http://www.ppic.org/content/pubs/report/R_1013SBR.pdf

Bishaw, Alemayehu. April 2009. "Adjusting Poverty Thresholds Based on Differences in Housing Costs: Applications in the American Community Survey, " poster presentation prepared for the Population Association of America Annual Conference.

Carrillo, Paul E. and Dirk W. Early, Edgar O. Olsen. June 24, 2012. "A Panel of Price Indices for Housing Services, Other Goods and All Goods for All Areas in the United States 1982-2010," Virginia Economics Online Papers 402, University of Virginia, Department of Economics.

Citro, Constance F., and Robert T. Michael (eds). 1995. Measuring Poverty: A New Approach. Washington, D.C.: National Academy Press.

Edwards, Ashley, Brian McKenzie, and Kathleen Short. 2014. , "Work-related expenses in the Supplemental Poverty Measure," Poverty Measurement Working Paper, http://www.census.gov/hhes/povmeas/publications/SGEworkexpense.pdf, U.S. Census Bureau.

Interagency Technical Working Group. 2010. "Observations from the Interagency Technical Working Group on Developing a Supplemental Poverty Measure." Available at <www.census.gov/hhes/www/poverty/SPM_TWGObservations.

Rapino, Melanie, Brian McKenzie and Mathew Marlay. 2010. "Research on Commuting Expenditures for the Supplemental Poverty Measure." Available from U.S. Census Bureau working papers.

Rapino, Melanie, Brian McKenzie and Mathew Marlay. 2011. Research on Commuting Expenditures and Geographic Adjustments in the Supplemental Poverty Measure. Paper presented at the Joint Statistical Meetings, August 2011.

Renwick, Trudi and Alemayehu Bishaw. 2013. Where are the Poor? Do Prices Matter? Supplemental Poverty Measure: Geographic Adjustments. Poster presented at the 2013 Population Association of America meetings. http://www.census.gov/hhes/www/poverty/publications/PAA_Where_are_the_Poor_Do_prices_matter.pdf

Renwick, Trudi. 2011. "Geographic Adjustments of Supplemental Poverty Measure Thresholds: Using the American Community Survey Five-Year Data on Housing Costs. Paper presented at the July 2011 Western Economic Association, San Diego, CA. Available from Census Bureau working papers.

Renwick, Trudi. 2009. "Alternative Geographic Adjustments of U.S. Poverty Thresholds: Impact on State Poverty Rates." Paper presented at the Joint Statistical Meetings, Washington, D.C. Available from Census Bureau working papers.

Short, Kathleen. 2013. "The Research Supplemental Poverty Measure: 2012." U.S. Census Bureau, Washington, D.C.

Short, Kathleen. 2001. "Where We Live: Geographic Differences in Poverty Thresholds," United States Bureau of the Census. Paper presented at the Annual Meeting of the Society of Government Economists, New Orleans, LA.

Short, Kathleen, Thesia Garner, David Johnson and Patricia Doyle. 1999. Experimental Poverty Measures: 1990 to 1997, U.S. Census Bureau, Current Population Reports, Consumer Income P60-205, Washington, D.C.: U.S. Government Printing Office.

Table 1: MRI and RPP Index Values; Thresholds for Two Adult/Two Child Renters: 2011

	Index Values					Thresholds for Two Adults/Two Chidren -		
	MRI	Overall RPP	Rent RPP	Food RPP	Apparel RPP	MRI	Overall RPP	Item-Specific RPP
Minimium	0.596	0.806	0.482	0.880	0.861	20,163	20,334	17,987
Maximum	1.725	1.231	1.931	1.223	1.272	34,310	31,053	38,359
Range	1.129	0.425	1.449	0.343	0.411	14,147	10,719	20,372
Akron, OH	0.905	0.887	0.797	0.964	0.936	24,028	22,366	22,342
Alabama Nonmetro	0.614	0.815	0.491	0.929	0.887	20,387	20,566	18,191
Alaska Nonmetro	1.148	0.994	1.155	0.977	0.932	27,072	25,072	26,919
Alaska Other Metro	1.187	1.104	1.427	1.125	0.909	27,565	27,834	31,396
Albany, GA	0.683	0.835	0.556	0.960	0.979	21,252	21,053	19,337
Albany-Schenectady-Troy, NY	1.043	0.998	1.052	0.993	0.907	25,759	25,172	25,720
Albuquerque, NM	0.874	0.968	0.930	0.990	0.915	23,640	24,416	24,176
Allentown-Bethlehem-Easton, PA-NJ	1.042	1.007	1.037	1.001	0.926	25,744	25,387	25,611
Altoona, PA	0.676	0.905	0.662	0.993	0.907	21,163	22,816	20,830
Amarillo, TX	0.820	0.937	0.829	0.965	0.995	22,969	23,633	22,817
Anderson, IN	0.792	0.887	0.662	0.956	0.975	22,611	22,381	20,635
Anderson, SC	0.712	0.888	0.656	0.966	0.998	21,611	22,389	20,650
Ann Arbor, MI	1.073	1.030	1.157	0.982	0.996	26,132	25,976	27,057
Anniston-Oxford, AL	0.676	0.833	0.527	0.966	0.998	21,163	21,005	19,033
Appleton, WI	0.799	0.932	0.804	0.956	0.975	22,700	23,497	22,406
Arizona Nonmetro	0.764	0.898	0.643	0.977	0.932	22,267	22,639	20,503
Arkansas Nonmetro	0.620	0.821	0.482	0.921	0.861	20,462	20,700	17,987
Arkansas Other Metro	0.717	0.827	0.596	0.944	0.929	21,670	20,867	19,657
Asheville, NC	0.845	0.930	0.859	0.953	0.957	23,282	23,465	23,056
Athens-Clarke County, GA	0.850	0.933	0.826	0.964	0.992	23,342	23,539	22,765
Atlanta-Sandy Springs-Marietta, GA	1.058	0.977	0.980	0.984	1.086	25,953	24,654	24,954
Atlantic City-Hammonton, NJ	1.235	1.090	1.121	1.086	1.014	28,162	27,501	27,389
Augusta-Richmond County, GA-SC	0.770	0.896	0.693	0.964	0.993	22,342	22,589	21,098
Austin-Round Rock-San Marcos, TX	1.119	0.994	1.101	0.966	0.998	26,714	25,058	26,234
Bakersfield-Delano, CA	0.885	0.977	0.976	0.991	0.915	23,774	24,635	24,761
Baltimore-Towson, MD	1.261	1.091	1.183	1.106	0.949	28,490	27,520	28,244
Bangor, ME	0.901	0.983	0.976	0.993	0.907	23,983	24,799	24,761
Barnstable Town, MA	1.351	1.042	1.241	0.996	0.927	29,624	26,288	28,135
Baton Rouge, LA	0.877	0.930	0.830	0.958	0.974	23,685	23,456	22,747
Beaumont-Port Arthur, TX	0.845	0.903	0.700	0.966	0.998	23,282	22,782	21,211
Bellingham, WA	0.964	0.990	1.046	0.991	0.915	24,774	24,961	25,630
Bend, OR	0.927	0.979	0.982	0.976	0.932	24,312	24,695	24,752
Billings, MT	0.812	0.958	0.864	0.990	0.916	22,864	24,154	23,357
Binghamton, NY	0.756	0.954	0.844	0.993	0.907	22,163	24,073	23,102
Birmingham-Hoover, AL	0.857	0.905	0.720	0.963	0.990	23,431	22,817	21,428
Bloomington, IN	0.851	0.936	0.904	0.948	0.953	23,357	23,616	23,576
Bloomington-Normal, IL	0.851	0.946	0.874	0.956	0.975	23,357	23,861	23,289
Boise City-Nampa, ID	0.833	0.954	0.858	0.990	0.916	23,133	24,051	23,274
Boston-Cambridge-Quincy, MA-NH	1.461	1.121	1.443	1.014	1.042	30,997	28,279	30,927
Boulder, CO	1.173	1.071	1.389	0.998	1.180	27,386	27,003	30,285
Bowling Green, KY	0.744	0.836	0.667	0.920	0.863	22,014	21,075	20,300
Bremerton-Silverdale, WA	1.055	1.045	1.108	1.062	1.183	25,908	26,362	27,233
Bridgeport-Stamford-Norwalk, CT	1.506	1.216	1.475	1.140	1.165	31,564	30,679	32,401
Brownsville-Harlingen, TX	0.712	0.846	0.577	0.966	0.998	21,611	21,349	19,659
Buffalo-Niagara Falls, NY	0.814	0.942	0.791	0.993	0.907	22,894	23,753	22,438
Burlington-South Burlington, VT	1.192	1.030	1.248	0.993	0.907	27,625	25,988	28,172
California Nonmetro	1.023	0.992	1.066	0.977	0.932	25,506	25,028	25,796
Canton-Massillon, OH	0.750	0.897	0.676	0.956	0.975	22,088	22,622	20,807
Cape Coral-Fort Myers, FL	1.083	0.981	1.033	0.966	0.998	26,267	24,750	25,385
Cedar Rapids, IA	0.790	0.909	0.744	0.951	0.963	22,596	22,936	21,614
Champaign-Urbana, IL	0.896	0.945	0.906	0.952	0.965	23,924	23,823	23,648

Table 1: MRI and RPP Index Values; Thresholds for Two Adult/Two Child Renters: 2011

	Index Values					Thresholds for Two Adults/Two Chidren -		
	MRI	Overall RPP	Rent RPP	Food RPP	Apparel RPP	MRI	Overall RPP	Item-Specific RPP
Charleston, WV	0.698	0.884	0.643	0.962	0.985	21,432	22,308	20,452
Charleston-North Charleston-Summerville, SC	0.987	0.964	0.948	0.966	0.998	25,058	24,315	24,321
Charlotte-Gastonia-Rock Hill, NC-SC	0.914	0.952	0.887	0.966	0.997	24,148	24,009	23,553
Chattanooga, TN-GA	0.786	0.909	0.730	0.964	0.992	22,536	22,924	21,562
Chicago-Joliet-Naperville, IL-IN-WI	1.110	1.075	1.209	1.063	1.120	26,595	27,107	28,444
Chico, CA	1.018	1.002	1.109	0.991	0.915	25,446	25,262	26,423
Cincinnati-Middletown, OH-KY-IN	0.864	0.930	0.828	1.024	0.924	23,521	23,459	23,164
Cleveland-Elyria-Mentor, OH	0.879	0.897	0.843	0.964	0.936	23,700	22,620	22,918
Coeur d'Alene, ID	0.823	0.951	0.866	0.976	0.932	22,998	23,983	23,292
Colorado Nonmetro	0.908	0.970	0.950	0.977	0.932	24,073	24,472	24,352
Colorado Other Metro	0.869	0.969	0.935	0.976	0.932	23,580	24,428	24,161
Colorado Springs, CO	0.935	0.987	1.033	0.990	0.915	24,401	24,891	25,472
Columbia, MO	0.790	0.926	0.802	0.955	0.971	22,596	23,354	22,376
Columbia, SC	0.864	0.930	0.818	0.962	0.986	23,521	23,454	22,639
Columbus, GA-AL	0.825	0.910	0.742	0.965	0.996	23,028	22,939	21,731
Columbus, OH	0.919	0.941	0.865	0.955	0.972	24,207	23,725	23,165
Connecticut Nonmetro	1.045	1.008	1.033	1.006	0.938	25,789	25,434	25,604
Connecticut Other Metro	1.176	1.007	1.097	0.993	0.909	27,431	25,409	26,281
Corpus Christi, TX	0.968	0.932	0.827	0.964	0.992	24,819	23,514	22,782
Crestview-Fort Walton Beach - Destin, FL	1.036	0.985	1.044	0.966	0.998	25,670	24,834	25,521
Dallas-Fort Worth-Arlington, TX	1.058	1.019	1.012	0.985	1.132	25,953	25,695	25,407
Danbury, CT	1.580	1.204	1.426	1.136	1.158	32,489	30,366	31,746
Davenport-Moline-Rock Island, IA-IL	0.782	0.917	0.752	0.955	0.972	22,491	23,118	21,750
Dayton, OH	0.826	0.918	0.773	0.955	0.972	23,043	23,148	22,010
Decatur, AL	0.646	0.864	0.576	0.966	0.998	20,790	21,779	19,658
Decatur, IL	0.737	0.899	0.676	0.956	0.975	21,924	22,671	20,803
Delaware Nonmetro	0.945	0.892	0.834	0.920	0.863	24,536	22,498	22,399
Deltona-Daytona Beach-Ormond Beach, FL	1.039	0.976	1.002	0.966	0.998	25,715	24,625	24,988
Denver-Aurora-Broomfield, CO	1.075	1.034	1.143	0.998	1.175	26,162	26,080	27,190
Des Moines-West Des Moines, IA	0.869	0.950	0.910	0.955	0.972	23,580	23,972	23,725
Detroit-Warren-Livonia, MI	0.976	0.992	0.930	0.982	0.996	24,924	25,011	24,206
Dover, DE	1.049	0.949	0.890	0.966	0.998	25,834	23,938	23,589
Duluth, MN-WI	0.837	0.927	0.834	0.952	0.964	23,177	23,378	22,746
Durham-Chapel Hill, NC	0.960	0.961	0.936	0.964	0.993	24,715	24,229	24,142
Eau Claire, WI	0.790	0.928	0.802	0.956	0.975	22,596	23,414	22,390
El Centro, CA	0.818	0.919	0.761	0.976	0.932	22,939	23,188	21,975
El Paso, TX	0.727	0.907	0.733	0.966	0.998	21,805	22,868	21,622
Erie, PA	0.783	0.928	0.745	0.993	0.907	22,506	23,406	21,864
Eugene-Springfield, OR	0.911	0.978	0.984	0.991	0.915	24,103	24,672	24,855
Evansville, IN-KY	0.839	0.913	0.758	0.953	0.968	23,207	23,030	21,808
Fargo, ND-MN	0.746	0.939	0.846	0.956	0.975	22,043	23,695	22,940
Farmington, NM	0.811	0.921	0.732	0.976	0.932	22,849	23,235	21,607
Fayetteville, NC	0.869	0.922	0.797	0.963	0.988	23,580	23,260	22,383
Fayetteville-Springdale-Rogers, AR-MO	0.789	0.911	0.735	0.965	0.996	22,581	22,981	21,631
Flint, MI	0.808	0.943	0.724	0.982	0.996	22,819	23,778	21,631
Florence-Muscle Shoals, AL	0.650	0.824	0.497	0.966	0.998	20,835	20,786	18,662
Florida Nonmetro	0.811	0.896	0.794	0.920	0.861	22,849	22,594	21,899
Fort Collins-Loveland, CO	0.936	0.993	1.075	0.991	0.915	24,416	25,047	25,993
Fort Smith, AR-OK	0.699	0.870	0.606	0.964	0.991	21,446	21,934	20,001
Fort Wayne, IN	0.762	0.917	0.741	0.956	0.975	22,237	23,119	21,620
Fresno, CA	0.960	0.978	0.985	0.991	0.915	24,715	24,677	24,872
Gainesville, FL	1.033	0.981	1.028	0.965	0.994	25,640	24,735	25,300
Georgia Nonmetro	0.651	0.838	0.543	0.921	0.862	20,850	21,126	18,758
Georgia Other Metro	0.808	0.871	0.768	0.920	0.863	22,819	21,979	21,567
Grand Rapids-Wyoming, MI	0.844	0.928	0.843	0.950	0.960	23,267	23,398	22,836
Greeley, CO	0.842	0.978	0.881	0.998	1.180	23,237	24,670	23,920
Green Bay, WI	0.811	0.922	0.809	0.951	0.961	22,849	23,263	22,412
Greensboro-High Point, NC	0.794	0.912	0.745	0.963	0.988	22,640	23,005	21,736

Table 1: MRI and RPP Index Values; Thresholds for Two Adult/Two Child Renters: 2011

	Index Values					**Thresholds for Two Adults/Two Chidren -**		
	MRI	**Overall RPP**	**Rent RPP**	**Food RPP**	**Apparel RPP**	**MRI**	**Overall RPP**	**Item-Specific RPP**
Greenville-Mauldin-Easley, SC	0.780	0.914	0.750	0.964	0.991	22,461	23,055	21,807
Gulfport-Biloxi, MS	0.996	0.932	0.830	0.964	0.992	25,177	23,517	22,816
Hagerstown-Martinsburg, MD-WV	0.920	1.050	0.914	1.131	1.075	24,222	26,488	25,206
Harrisburg-Carlisle, PA	0.938	0.972	0.917	0.993	0.907	24,446	24,507	24,017
Harrisonburg, VA	0.867	0.926	0.938	0.920	0.863	23,551	23,364	23,698
Hartford-West Hartford-East Hartford, CT	1.170	1.016	1.138	0.995	0.913	27,356	25,623	26,823
Hawaii Nonmetro	1.393	1.044	1.325	0.976	0.932	30,147	26,328	29,042
Hickory-Lenoir-Morganton, NC	0.690	0.899	0.688	0.966	0.998	21,342	22,664	21,057
Holland-Grand Haven, MI	0.836	0.952	0.912	0.956	0.975	23,163	24,017	23,770
Honolulu, HI	1.614	1.231	1.781	1.223	1.143	32,922	31,053	36,826
Houston-Sugar Land-Baytown, TX	1.017	1.010	1.001	1.004	1.057	25,431	25,466	25,325
Huntington-Ashland, WV-KY-OH	0.725	0.868	0.608	0.966	0.998	21,775	21,881	20,048
Huntsville, AL	0.755	0.914	0.719	0.966	0.998	22,148	23,061	21,441
Idaho Nonmetro	0.705	0.928	0.735	0.977	0.932	21,521	23,396	21,650
Idaho Other Metro	0.714	0.919	0.735	0.976	0.932	21,641	23,166	21,653
Illinois Nonmetro	0.692	0.825	0.604	0.915	0.867	21,357	20,800	19,481
Indiana Nonmetro	0.718	0.832	0.633	0.920	0.879	21,685	20,980	19,890
Indiana Other Metro	0.813	0.911	0.769	0.956	0.957	22,879	22,967	21,951
Indianapolis-Carmel, IN	0.904	0.945	0.883	0.955	0.973	24,013	23,839	23,397
Iowa City, IA	0.894	0.959	0.980	0.952	0.965	23,894	24,194	24,573
Iowa Nonmetro	0.651	0.833	0.588	0.914	0.863	20,850	21,019	19,262
Iowa Other Metro	0.804	0.915	0.812	0.946	0.948	22,760	23,069	22,409
Jackson, MI	0.811	0.906	0.732	0.956	0.975	22,849	22,863	21,511
Jackson, MS	0.911	0.919	0.769	0.964	0.991	24,103	23,182	22,045
Jacksonville, FL	1.045	0.977	1.010	0.965	0.997	25,789	24,638	25,083
Jacksonville, NC	0.854	0.957	0.920	0.966	0.998	23,386	24,133	23,965
Janesville, WI	0.858	0.929	0.812	0.956	0.975	23,446	23,444	22,514
Johnson City, TN	0.664	0.882	0.640	0.966	0.998	21,014	22,253	20,452
Johnstown, PA	0.611	0.842	0.508	0.993	0.907	20,342	21,230	18,902
Joplin, MO	0.706	0.874	0.611	0.956	0.975	21,536	22,039	19,989
Kalamazoo-Portage, MI	0.827	0.934	0.830	0.956	0.975	23,058	23,550	22,732
Kankakee-Bradley, IL	0.858	0.985	0.819	1.063	1.121	23,446	24,854	23,557
Kansas City, MO-KS	0.918	0.928	0.861	0.880	1.019	24,192	23,416	22,613
Kansas Nonmetro	0.668	0.820	0.571	0.914	0.863	21,059	20,673	19,056
Kentucky Nonmetro	0.608	0.843	0.524	0.922	0.866	20,312	21,266	18,533
Kentucky Other Metro	0.681	0.863	0.634	0.953	0.958	21,223	21,772	20,235
Killeen-Temple-Fort Hood, TX	0.863	0.933	0.827	0.964	0.993	23,506	23,528	22,780
Kingsport-Bristol-Bristol, TN-VA	0.644	0.875	0.607	0.966	0.998	20,760	22,060	20,043
Kingston, NY	1.220	1.038	1.277	0.993	0.907	27,983	26,184	28,536
Knoxville, TN	0.813	0.916	0.746	0.966	0.998	22,879	23,113	21,783
La Crosse, WI-MN	0.807	0.939	0.850	0.956	0.975	22,804	23,693	22,989
Lafayette, LA	0.802	0.918	0.741	0.966	0.998	22,745	23,148	21,725
Lake Charles, LA	0.799	0.884	0.637	0.965	0.995	22,700	22,301	20,406
Lakeland-Winter Haven, FL	0.952	0.955	0.914	0.966	0.998	24,625	24,096	23,886
Lancaster, PA	0.974	0.989	1.004	0.993	0.907	24,894	24,943	25,109
Lansing-East Lansing, MI	0.913	0.954	0.923	0.956	0.975	24,133	24,049	23,907
Laredo, TX	0.820	0.891	0.699	0.966	0.998	22,969	22,481	21,190
Las Cruces, NM	0.708	0.924	0.742	0.991	0.915	21,566	23,298	21,825
Las Vegas-Paradise, NV	1.181	1.008	1.151	0.991	0.915	27,490	25,433	26,951
Lawrence, KS	0.913	0.958	0.947	0.956	0.975	24,133	24,168	24,206
Lawton, OK	0.763	0.911	0.732	0.966	0.998	22,252	22,973	21,608
Leominster-Fitchburg-Gardner, MA	1.023	1.043	0.999	1.014	1.040	25,506	26,307	25,352
Lexington-Fayette, KY	0.804	0.933	0.805	0.966	0.998	22,760	23,532	22,519
Little Rock-North Little Rock-Conway, AR	0.827	0.919	0.761	0.965	0.995	23,058	23,171	21,960
Longview, TX	0.796	0.914	0.763	0.959	0.976	22,670	23,065	21,920
Los Angeles-Long Beach-Santa Ana, CA	1.552	1.172	1.739	1.042	1.039	32,146	29,559	34,835
Louisiana Nonmetro	0.650	0.821	0.514	0.927	0.882	20,835	20,718	18,462
Louisiana Other Metro	0.774	0.892	0.665	0.965	0.994	22,387	22,488	20,753

Table 1: MRI and RPP Index Values; Thresholds for Two Adult/Two Child Renters: 2011

		Index Values					Thresholds for Two Adults/Two Chidren -	
	MRI	Overall RPP	Rent RPP	Food RPP	Apparel RPP	MRI	Overall RPP	Item-Specific RPP
Louisville/Jefferson County, KY-IN	0.802	0.916	0.756	0.962	0.987	22,745	23,095	21,870
Lubbock, TX	0.850	0.943	0.859	0.965	0.997	23,342	23,795	23,198
Lynchburg, VA	0.724	0.908	0.718	0.964	0.993	21,760	22,895	21,419
Macon, GA	0.770	0.875	0.648	0.961	0.982	22,342	22,072	20,501
Madera-Chowchilla, CA	0.945	0.973	0.955	0.991	0.915	24,536	24,528	24,490
Madison, WI	1.033	0.980	1.109	0.953	0.966	25,640	24,726	26,202
Maine Nonmetro	0.762	0.954	0.770	0.993	0.907	22,237	24,060	22,182
Maine Other Metro	0.910	0.974	0.921	0.994	0.917	24,088	24,576	24,095
Maryland Nonmetro	1.023	0.918	0.896	0.920	0.862	25,506	23,152	23,171
Maryland Other Metro	0.644	0.890	0.666	0.966	0.998	20,760	22,438	20,775
Massachusetts Other Metro	0.965	1.000	0.978	0.999	0.949	24,789	25,227	24,885
McAllen-Edinburg-Mission, TX	0.733	0.836	0.547	0.966	0.998	21,879	21,097	19,285
Medford, OR	0.926	0.984	1.014	0.991	0.915	24,297	24,822	25,230
Memphis, TN-MS-AR	0.904	0.931	0.814	0.965	0.994	24,013	23,488	22,625
Merced, CA	0.863	0.961	0.899	0.991	0.915	23,506	24,246	23,787
Miami-Fort Lauderdale-Pompano Beach, FL	1.321	1.058	1.333	1.021	1.038	29,251	26,696	29,591
Michigan City-La Porte, IN	0.813	0.847	0.751	0.914	0.862	22,879	21,364	21,310
Michigan Nonmetro	0.739	0.862	0.703	0.923	0.886	21,954	21,731	20,804
Michigan Other Metro	0.789	0.893	0.709	0.951	0.961	22,581	22,518	21,169
Midland, TX	1.039	0.966	0.957	0.966	0.998	25,715	24,376	24,424
Milwaukee-Waukesha-West Allis, WI	0.952	0.957	1.005	0.905	1.025	24,625	24,129	24,602
Minneapolis-St. Paul-Bloomington, MN-WI	1.093	1.036	1.140	1.011	0.924	26,386	26,129	26,976
Minnesota Nonmetro	0.730	0.849	0.686	0.914	0.863	21,834	21,421	20,498
Minnesota Other Metro	0.833	0.925	0.853	0.946	0.949	23,133	23,325	22,928
Mississippi Nonmetro	0.638	0.809	0.497	0.920	0.861	20,685	20,410	18,176
Mississippi Other Metro	0.810	0.887	0.740	0.947	0.941	22,834	22,384	21,505
Missouri Nonmetro	0.635	0.808	0.548	0.914	0.863	20,641	20,383	18,762
Missouri Other Metro	0.708	0.836	0.638	0.929	0.904	21,566	21,091	20,053
Mobile, AL	0.808	0.883	0.656	0.966	0.998	22,819	22,271	20,658
Modesto, CA	1.057	0.995	1.075	0.991	0.915	25,938	25,103	26,003
Monroe, LA	0.719	0.864	0.586	0.963	0.988	21,700	21,788	19,743
Monroe, MI	0.877	0.971	0.830	0.982	0.996	23,685	24,486	22,951
Montana Nonmetro	0.733	0.927	0.721	0.977	0.932	21,879	23,380	21,481
Montana Other Metro	0.804	0.954	0.860	0.984	0.924	22,760	24,053	23,265
Montgomery, AL	0.851	0.902	0.712	0.965	0.996	23,357	22,756	21,352
Muskegon-Norton Shores, MI	0.756	0.896	0.698	0.956	0.975	22,163	22,608	21,085
Myrtle Beach-North Myrtle Beach-Conway, S(	0.929	0.953	0.900	0.966	0.998	24,327	24,030	23,718
Napa, CA	1.487	1.193	1.651	1.161	1.272	31,325	30,088	34,883
Naples-Marco Island, FL	1.223	1.008	1.234	0.966	0.998	28,013	25,432	27,902
Nashville-Davidson--Murfreesboro--Franklin,	0.924	0.952	0.894	0.965	0.995	24,267	24,000	23,628
Nebraska Nonmetro	0.688	0.830	0.597	0.914	0.863	21,312	20,940	19,384
Nebraska Other Metro	0.807	0.931	0.822	0.954	0.970	22,804	23,475	22,616
Nevada Nonmetro	0.940	0.960	0.888	0.979	0.929	24,476	24,201	23,588
Nevada Other Metro	1.038	1.001	1.088	0.976	0.932	25,700	25,250	26,079
New Hampshire Nonmetro	1.089	1.014	1.141	0.993	0.912	26,341	25,571	26,847
New Hampshire Other Metro	1.230	1.100	1.303	1.013	1.035	28,102	27,742	29,153
New Haven, CT	1.304	1.150	1.281	1.103	1.110	29,027	29,006	29,639
New Mexico Nonmetro	0.686	0.896	0.649	0.978	0.931	21,282	22,602	20,579
New Orleans-Metairie-Kenner, LA	1.092	0.989	1.067	0.966	0.998	26,371	24,943	25,807
New York Nonmetro	0.794	0.953	0.806	0.993	0.907	22,640	24,032	22,628
New York-Northern New Jersey-Long Island, I	1.368	1.216	1.593	1.099	1.123	29,833	30,672	33,528
Niles-Benton Harbor, MI	0.748	0.908	0.714	0.956	0.975	22,058	22,893	21,285
North Carolina Nonmetro	0.707	0.853	0.627	0.927	0.881	21,551	21,506	19,870
North Carolina Other Metro	0.825	0.903	0.737	0.960	0.981	23,028	22,769	21,604
North Dakota Nonmetro	0.596	0.839	0.600	0.914	0.863	20,163	21,162	19,410
North Dakota Other Metro	0.740	0.938	0.823	0.956	0.975	21,969	23,653	22,656
Norwich-New London, CT-RI (RI portion recoc	1.204	1.021	1.183	0.993	0.907	27,774	25,762	27,356
Ocala, FL	0.924	0.940	0.858	0.966	0.998	24,267	23,701	23,181

Table 1: MRI and RPP Index Values; Thresholds for Two Adult/Two Child Renters: 2011

	Index Values					Thresholds for Two Adults/Two Chidren -		
	MRI	**Overall RPP**	**Rent RPP**	**Food RPP**	**Apparel RPP**	**MRI**	**Overall RPP**	**Item-Specific RPP**
Ocean City, NJ	1.142	1.098	1.163	1.086	1.014	26,998	27,705	27,920
Ogden-Clearfield, UT	0.857	0.959	0.880	0.990	0.915	23,431	24,186	23,554
Ohio Nonmetro	0.700	0.827	0.622	0.921	0.879	21,461	20,868	19,765
Ohio Other Metro	0.693	0.864	0.605	0.955	0.971	21,372	21,787	19,900
Oklahoma City, OK	0.818	0.923	0.774	0.964	0.993	22,939	23,282	22,112
Oklahoma Nonmetro	0.651	0.846	0.551	0.924	0.872	20,850	21,345	18,894
Olympia, WA	1.044	1.051	1.135	1.062	1.183	25,774	26,499	27,570
Omaha-Council Bluffs, NE-IA	0.910	0.946	0.890	0.955	0.971	24,088	23,849	23,470
Oregon Nonmetro	0.783	0.943	0.825	0.976	0.932	22,506	23,784	22,782
Orlando-Kissimmee-Sanford, FL	1.150	1.001	1.122	0.966	0.998	27,102	25,249	26,496
Oshkosh-Neenah, WI	0.768	0.931	0.804	0.956	0.975	22,312	23,472	22,415
Oxnard-Thousand Oaks-Ventura, CA	1.655	1.137	1.740	0.954	1.048	33,430	28,678	34,207
Palm Bay-Melbourne-Titusville, FL	1.025	0.977	1.009	0.966	0.998	25,535	24,646	25,076
Panama City-Lynn Haven-Panama City Beach,	1.004	0.980	1.018	0.966	0.998	25,267	24,710	25,187
Pennsylvania Nonmetro	0.698	0.920	0.683	0.990	0.905	21,432	23,200	21,075
Pensacola-Ferry Pass-Brent, FL	0.920	0.952	0.900	0.966	0.998	24,222	24,018	23,710
Peoria, IL	0.815	0.919	0.756	0.955	0.972	22,909	23,174	21,803
Philadelphia-Camden-Wilmington, PA-NJ-DE-	1.164	1.096	1.159	1.086	1.014	27,281	27,652	27,864
Phoenix-Mesa-Glendale, AZ	1.039	1.020	1.063	0.977	1.078	25,715	25,732	25,918
Pittsburgh, PA	0.819	0.923	0.785	1.019	0.919	22,954	23,279	22,577
Port St. Lucie, FL	1.114	0.986	1.048	0.966	0.998	26,655	24,863	25,570
Portland-South Portland, ME	1.113	1.015	1.124	0.994	0.917	26,640	25,603	26,635
Portland-Vancouver-Hillsboro, OR-WA	0.995	1.006	1.105	0.973	1.185	25,162	25,364	26,542
Poughkeepsie-Newburgh-Middletown, NY	1.310	1.216	1.383	1.148	1.175	29,102	30,663	31,310
Prescott, AZ	0.955	0.978	0.977	0.976	0.932	24,655	24,667	24,690
Providence-Fall River-Warwick, RI-MA	1.077	1.010	1.066	0.996	0.927	26,192	25,464	25,934
Provo-Orem, UT	0.837	0.973	0.958	0.990	0.915	23,177	24,552	24,530
Pueblo, CO	0.755	0.928	0.762	0.991	0.915	22,148	23,401	22,075
Punta Gorda, FL	1.007	0.973	0.990	0.966	0.998	25,312	24,551	24,836
Racine, WI	0.871	0.938	0.897	0.905	1.025	23,610	23,653	23,245
Raleigh-Cary, NC	0.993	0.962	0.937	0.966	0.998	25,132	24,274	24,177
Reading, PA	0.939	0.971	0.915	0.993	0.907	24,461	24,482	23,994
Reno-Sparks, NV	1.114	1.003	1.131	0.990	0.915	26,655	25,294	26,699
Richmond, VA	1.024	0.974	1.007	0.964	0.991	25,520	24,577	25,034
Riverside-San Bernardino-Ontario, CA	1.232	1.074	1.298	0.954	1.048	28,132	27,097	28,666
Roanoke, VA	0.814	0.922	0.795	0.960	0.981	22,894	23,250	22,338
Rochester, NY	0.933	0.984	0.978	0.993	0.907	24,386	24,819	24,791
Rochester-Dover, NH-ME (Maine portion not	1.126	1.079	1.214	1.012	1.027	26,804	27,205	28,018
Rockford, IL	0.849	0.925	0.797	0.956	0.975	23,327	23,341	22,321
Sacramento--Arden-Arcade--Roseville, CA	1.181	1.026	1.285	0.991	0.915	27,490	25,884	28,633
Saginaw-Saginaw Township North, MI	0.783	0.899	0.705	0.956	0.975	22,506	22,681	21,174
Salem, OR	0.838	0.974	0.909	0.973	1.186	23,193	24,559	24,085
Salinas, CA	1.313	1.061	1.571	0.991	0.915	29,147	26,772	32,214
Salisbury, MD	1.027	0.916	0.905	0.920	0.863	25,565	23,108	23,289
Salt Lake City, UT	0.962	0.993	1.068	0.990	0.916	24,744	25,048	25,906
San Antonio-New Braunfels, TX	0.948	0.946	0.875	0.964	0.992	24,565	23,862	23,375
San Diego-Carlsbad-San Marcos, CA	1.506	1.170	1.718	1.062	1.112	31,564	29,510	34,811
San Francisco-Oakland-Fremont, CA	1.661	1.215	1.877	1.161	1.272	33,504	30,643	37,714
San Jose-Sunnyvale-Santa Clara, CA	1.725	1.217	1.931	1.158	1.265	34,310	30,702	38,359
San Luis Obispo-Paso Robles, CA	1.339	1.060	1.536	0.991	0.915	29,475	26,732	31,773
Santa Barbara-Santa Maria-Goleta, CA	1.567	1.074	1.753	0.991	0.915	32,325	27,100	34,499
Santa Cruz-Watsonville, CA	1.649	1.208	1.722	1.161	1.272	33,355	30,470	35,769
Santa Fe, NM	1.075	0.993	1.072	0.991	0.915	26,162	25,035	25,966
Santa Rosa-Petaluma, CA	1.423	1.188	1.556	1.161	1.272	30,520	29,965	33,693
Sarasota-Bradenton-Venice, FL	1.133	1.005	1.159	0.966	0.998	26,893	25,353	26,958
Savannah, GA	0.986	0.960	0.931	0.966	0.998	25,043	24,215	24,101
Scranton--Wilkes-Barre, PA	0.758	0.918	0.713	0.993	0.907	22,193	23,146	21,468
Seattle-Tacoma-Bellevue, WA	1.192	1.075	1.305	1.062	1.183	27,625	27,101	29,703

Table 1: MRI and RPP Index Values; Thresholds for Two Adult/Two Child Renters: 2011

	Index Values					Thresholds for Two Adults/Two Chidren -		
	MRI	Overall RPP	Rent RPP	Food RPP	Apparel RPP	MRI	Overall RPP	Item-Specific RPP
Sebastian-Vero Beach, FL	1.018	0.940	0.989	0.920	0.863	25,446	23,717	24,344
Shreveport-Bossier City, LA	0.818	0.910	0.730	0.964	0.993	22,939	22,962	21,567
Sioux Falls, SD	0.795	0.936	0.836	0.955	0.971	22,655	23,609	22,802
South Bend-Mishawaka, IN-MI	0.851	0.924	0.787	0.956	0.975	23,357	23,306	22,202
South Carolina Nonmetro	0.687	0.835	0.604	0.922	0.868	21,297	21,052	19,533
South Dakota Nonmetro	0.626	0.806	0.522	0.914	0.863	20,536	20,334	18,438
South Dakota Other Metro	0.785	0.912	0.784	0.947	0.952	22,521	22,995	22,067
Spartanburg, SC	0.712	0.893	0.676	0.966	0.998	21,611	22,525	20,904
Spokane, WA	0.854	0.959	0.885	0.991	0.915	23,386	24,189	23,619
Springfield, IL	0.817	0.928	0.783	0.956	0.975	22,924	23,403	22,144
Springfield, MA-CT (Connecticut portion not i	0.975	0.975	0.936	0.993	0.907	24,909	24,583	24,265
Springfield, MO	0.742	0.896	0.702	0.954	0.968	21,984	22,603	21,112
Springfield, OH	0.780	0.888	0.660	0.956	0.975	22,461	22,394	20,609
St. Cloud, MN	0.807	0.937	0.849	0.956	0.975	22,804	23,630	22,973
St. Louis, MO-IL	0.917	0.887	0.849	0.952	0.967	24,177	22,381	22,936
Stockton, CA	1.102	1.012	1.174	0.991	0.915	26,505	25,520	27,242
Syracuse, NY	0.871	0.964	0.884	0.993	0.907	23,610	24,307	23,611
Tallahassee, FL	1.018	0.963	0.956	0.963	0.988	25,446	24,295	24,381
Tampa-St. Petersburg-Clearwater, FL	1.106	0.989	1.101	0.987	0.949	26,550	24,941	26,331
Tennessee Nonmetro	0.637	0.833	0.546	0.923	0.869	20,670	21,006	18,819
Tennessee Other Metro	0.758	0.863	0.695	0.940	0.920	22,193	21,768	20,862
Texas Nonmetro	0.714	0.864	0.596	0.924	0.872	21,641	21,793	19,451
Texas Other Metro	0.845	0.929	0.803	0.964	0.993	23,282	23,421	22,479
Toledo, OH	0.787	0.901	0.716	0.954	0.969	22,551	22,732	21,285
Topeka, KS	0.782	0.891	0.705	0.949	0.957	22,491	22,481	21,093
Trenton-Ewing, NJ	1.331	1.114	1.313	1.045	0.997	29,371	28,099	29,478
Tucson, AZ	0.940	0.974	0.964	0.991	0.915	24,476	24,575	24,602
Tulsa, OK	0.833	0.914	0.738	0.965	0.994	23,133	23,051	21,669
Tuscaloosa, AL	0.831	0.893	0.698	0.963	0.990	23,103	22,527	21,155
Utah Nonmetro	0.689	0.925	0.724	0.977	0.932	21,327	23,330	21,512
Utah Other Metro	0.799	0.943	0.837	0.976	0.932	22,700	23,775	22,928
Utica-Rome, NY	0.758	0.933	0.763	0.993	0.907	22,193	23,532	22,097
Valdosta, GA	0.776	0.833	0.680	0.920	0.863	22,416	21,012	20,466
Vallejo-Fairfield, CA	1.329	1.175	1.466	1.161	1.272	29,341	29,639	32,562
Vermont Nonmetro	0.962	0.990	1.033	0.993	0.907	24,744	24,970	25,480
Vermont Other Metro	0.895	0.937	0.801	0.993	0.907	23,909	23,624	22,565
Victoria, TX	0.862	0.902	0.725	0.958	0.975	23,491	22,741	21,432
Vineland-Millville-Bridgeton, NJ	1.110	1.045	0.942	1.086	1.014	26,595	26,357	25,155
Virginia Beach-Norfolk-Newport News, VA-NC	1.095	1.001	1.128	0.966	0.998	26,416	25,251	26,573
Virginia Nonmetro	0.689	0.888	0.653	0.929	0.870	21,327	22,406	20,200
Virginia Other Metro	0.833	0.932	0.863	0.953	0.956	23,133	23,499	23,104
Visalia-Porterville, CA	0.832	0.957	0.879	0.991	0.915	23,118	24,137	23,545
Waco, TX	0.877	0.921	0.776	0.966	0.998	23,685	23,231	22,162
Warner Robins, GA	0.877	0.918	0.756	0.966	0.998	23,685	23,156	21,911
Washington Nonmetro	0.806	0.958	0.855	0.987	0.966	22,790	24,160	23,276
Washington Other Metro	0.848	0.969	0.928	0.984	0.924	23,312	24,433	24,118
Washington-Arlington-Alexandria, DC-VA-MD	1.545	1.209	1.703	1.131	1.075	32,057	30,482	35,088
Waterbury, CT	1.085	1.109	1.000	1.123	1.139	26,281	27,959	26,282
Waterloo-Cedar Falls, IA	0.745	0.910	0.771	0.949	0.956	22,028	22,955	21,915
Wausau, WI	0.780	0.924	0.771	0.956	0.975	22,461	23,305	21,998
West Virginia Nonmetro	0.607	0.836	0.503	0.921	0.861	20,297	21,083	18,244
West Virginia Other Metro	0.714	0.912	0.698	1.004	0.992	21,641	22,995	21,457
Wichita, KS	0.781	0.914	0.739	0.955	0.973	22,476	23,044	21,582
Winston-Salem, NC	0.765	0.918	0.746	0.966	0.998	22,282	23,142	21,787
Wisconsin Nonmetro	0.757	0.859	0.729	0.914	0.863	22,178	21,657	21,033
Wisconsin Other Metro	0.850	0.964	0.865	0.997	0.992	23,342	24,314	23,498
Worcester, MA-CT (Connecticut portion not i	1.098	1.061	1.095	1.013	1.035	26,446	26,749	26,544
Wyoming Nonmetro	0.782	0.959	0.874	0.977	0.932	22,491	24,187	23,398

Table 1: MRI and RPP Index Values; Thresholds for Two Adult/Two Child Renters: 2011

	Index Values					Thresholds for Two Adults/Two Chidren -		
	MRI	Overall RPP	Rent RPP	Food RPP	Apparel RPP	MRI	Overall RPP	Item-Specific RPP
Wyoming Other Metro	0.773	0.959	0.879	0.991	0.915	22,372	24,190	23,538
Yakima, WA	0.773	0.948	0.828	0.991	0.915	22,372	23,902	22,899
York-Hanover, PA	0.910	0.966	0.894	0.993	0.907	24,088	24,360	23,730
Youngstown-Warren-Boardman, OH-PA	0.708	0.880	0.637	0.956	0.975	21,566	22,201	20,314

Sources: MRI index from the American Community Survey 2007-2011. RPP index provided by the Bureau of Economic Analysis.

Table 2a: SPM Poverty Rates by Selected Characteristics: 2011

	Median Rent Index	SE	RPP Indices		SE		Difference MRI minus RPP	SE
TOTAL	16.1	0.2	Overall	15.6	0.2	*	0.5	0.1
	16.1	0.2	Item-specific	16.4	0.2	*	-0.3	0.1
REGION								
Northeast	15	0.4	Overall	15.5	0.4	*	-0.5	0.1
Midwest	12.8	0.3	Overall	12.5	0.3	*	0.3	0.1
South	16	0.3	Overall	15.3	0.3	*	0.6	0.1
West	20	0.4	Overall	18.8	0.4	*	1.2	0.1
Northeast	15	0.4	Item-specific	16.7	0.4	*	-1.7	0.2
Midwest	12.8	0.3	Item-specific	12.3	0.3	*	0.4	0.1
South	16	0.3	Item-specific	15	0.3	*	1.0	0.1
West	20	0.4	Item-specific	22	0.4	*	-2.0	0.1
AGE								
Children	18	0.3	Overall	17.4	0.3	*	0.6	0.1
Nonelderly adults	15.5	0.2	Overall	15	0.2	*	0.5	0.1
Elderly	15.1	0.3	Overall	14.7	0.3	*	0.3	0.1
Children	18	0.3	Item-specific	18.5	0.3	*	-0.4	0.1
Nonelderly adults	15.5	0.2	Item-specific	15.8	0.2	*	-0.3	0.1
Elderly	15.1	0.3	Item-specific	15.3	0.3		-0.2	0.1
METRO/NONMETRO								
Metro - In principal city	21.6	0.4	Overall	21	0.4	*	0.6	0.1
Metro - outside principal city	13.4	0.2	Overall	12.8	0.2	*	0.5	0.1
Nonmetro	13.4	0.5	Overall	13.2	0.4	*	0.2	0.1
Metro - In principal citiy	21.6	0.4	Item-specific	22.6	0.4	*	-1.0	0.1
Metro - outside principal city	13.4	0.2	Item-specific	13.8	0.2	*	-0.4	0.1
Nonmetro	13.4	0.5	Item-specific	11.9	0.4	*	1.6	0.1
TENURE								
Owner with mortgage	8.1	0.2	Overall	7.7	0.2	*	0.4	0.1
Owner no mortgage	13	0.3	Overall	12.9	0.3	*	0.2	0.1
Renter	29.3	0.4	Overall	28.4	0.4	*	0.9	0.1
Owner with mortgage	8.1	0.2	Item-specific	8.4	0.2	*	-0.3	0.1
Owner no mortgage	13	0.3	Item-specific	12.8	0.3	*	0.3	0.1
Renter	29.3	0.4	Item-specific	30	0.4	*	-0.8	0.1

* Difference is statistically significant at the 90 percent confidence level.

Source: 2012 Current Population Survey Annual Social and Economic Supplement.

Table 2b: Distribution of the Population by Selected Demographic Characteristics : 2011

REGION		Share	SE		Share	SE		Difference	SE
Northeast	Total Population	17.8	0.0	MRI	16.6	0.4	*	1.2	0.4
Midwest	Total Population	21.4	0.0	MRI	17	0.4	*	4.4	0.4
South	Total Population	37.3	0.0	MRI	37.1	0.6		0.2	0.6
West	Total Population	23.5	0.0	MRI	29.3	0.5	*	-5.8	0.5
Northeast	Total Population	17.8	0.0	overall RPP	17.7	0.4		0.1	0.4
Midwest	Total Population	21.4	0.0	overall RPP	17.2	0.4	*	4.2	0.4
South	Total Population	37.3	0.0	overall RPP	36.7	0.6		0.5	0.6
West	Total Population	23.5	0.0	overall RPP	28.4	0.5	*	-4.9	0.5
Northeast	Total Population	17.8	0.0	item-specific RPP	18.1	0.4		-0.3	0.4
Midwest	Total Population	21.4	0.0	item-specific RPP	16.1	0.4	*	5.3	0.4
South	Total Population	37.3	0.0	item-specific RPP	34.2	0.6	*	3.1	0.6
West	Total Population	23.5	0.0	item-specific RPP	31.6	0.5	*	-8.1	0.5
Northeast	MRI	16.6	0.4	overall RPP	17.7	0.4	*	-1.1	0.1
Midwest	MRI	17	0.4	overall RPP	17.2	0.4	*	-0.2	0.1
South	MRI	37.1	0.6	overall RPP	36.7	0.6	*	0.3	0.2
West	MRI	29.3	0.5	overall RPP	28.4	0.5	*	1.0	0.2
Northeast	MRI	16.6	0.4	item-specific RPP	18.1	0.4	*	-1.5	0.1
Midwest	MRI	17	0.4	item-specific RPP	16.1	0.4	*	0.9	0.1
South	MRI	37.1	0.6	item-specific RPP	34.2	0.6	*	2.9	0.2
West	MRI	29.3	0.5	item-specific RPP	31.6	0.5	*	-2.3	0.2
AGE									
Children	Total Population	24	0.0	MRI	26.9	0.3	*	-2.9	0.3
Nonelderly adults	Total Population	62.6	0.0	MRI	60.5	0.3	*	2.1	0.3
Elderly	Total Population	13.4	0.0	MRI	12.6	0.3	*	0.8	0.3
Children	Total Population	24	0.0	overall RPP	26.9	0.3	*	-2.9	0.3
Nonelderly adults	Total Population	62.6	0.0	overall RPP	60.4	0.3	*	2.2	0.3
Elderly	Total Population	13.4	0.0	overall RPP	12.7	0.3	*	0.7	0.3
Children	Total Population	24	0.0	item-specific RPP	27.1	0.3	*	-3.1	0.3
Nonelderly adults	Total Population	62.6	0.0	item-specific RPP	60.4	0.3	*	2.1	0.3
Elderly	Total Population	13.4	0.0	item-specific RPP	12.5	0.2	*	0.9	0.2
Children	MRI	26.9	0.3	overall RPP	26.9	0.3		0.1	0.1
Nonelderly adults	MRI	60.5	0.3	overall RPP	60.4	0.3		0.1	0.1
Elderly	MRI	12.6	0.3	overall RPP	12.7	0.3		-0.1	0.1
Children	MRI	26.9	0.3	item-specific RPP	27.1	0.3		-0.1	0.1
Nonelderly adults	MRI	60.5	0.3	item-specific RPP	60.4	0.3		0.0	0.1
Elderly	MRI	12.6	0.3	item-specific RPP	12.5	0.2		0.1	0.1

Table 2b: Distribution of the Population by Selected Demographic Characteristics : 2011

		Share	SE		Share	SE		Difference	SE
METRO/NONMETRO									
Metro - In principal city	Total Population	32.5	0.4	MRI	43.7	0.7	*	-11.3	0.6
Metro - outside principal city	Total Population	52.2	0.5	MRI	43.4	0.7	*	8.8	0.6
Nonmetro	Total Population	15.3	0.5	MRI	12.8	0.6	*	2.5	0.4
Metro - In principal city	Total Population	32.5	0.4	overall RPP	43.9	0.7	*	-11.4	0.6
Metro - outside principal city	Total Population	52.2	0.5	overall RPP	43	0.7	*	9.1	0.6
Nonmetro	Total Population	15.3	0.5	overall RPP	13	0.6	*	2.3	0.4
Metro - In principal city	Total Population	32.5	0.4	item-specific RPP	44.9	0.7	*	-12.4	0.6
Metro - outside principal city	Total Population	52.2	0.5	item-specific RPP	44	0.7	*	8.2	0.6
Nonmetro	Total Population	15.3	0.5	item-specific RPP	11.1	0.5	*	4.2	0.4
Metro - In principal city	MRI	43.7	0.7	overall RPP	43.9	0.7		-0.2	0.2
Metro - outside principal city	MRI	43.4	0.7	overall RPP	43	0.7	*	0.4	0.2
Nonmetro	MRI	12.8	0.6	overall RPP	13	0.6	*	-0.2	0.1
Metro - In principal city	MRI	43.7	0.7	item-specific RPP	44.9	0.7	*	-1.2	0.2
Metro - outside principal city	MRI	43.4	0.7	item-specific RPP	44	0.7	*	-0.6	0.2
Nonmetro	MRI	12.8	0.6	item-specific RPP	11.1	0.5	*	1.7	0.1
TENURE									
Owner with mortgage	Total Population	44.3	0.3	MRI	22.4	0.5	*	21.8	0.5
Owner no mortgage	Total Population	23.8	0.2	MRI	19.3	0.5	*	4.5	0.4
Renter	Total Population	32	0.2	MRI	58.3	0.6	*	-26.3	0.6
Owner with mortgage	Total Population	44.3	0.3	overall RPP	22	0.5	*	22.2	0.5
Owner no mortgage	Total Population	23.8	0.2	overall RPP	19.7	0.4	*	4.1	0.4
Renter	Total Population	32	0.2	overall RPP	58.3	0.6	*	-26.3	0.5
Owner with mortgage	Total Population	44.3	0.3	item-specific RPP	22.8	0.5	*	21.4	0.5
Owner no mortgage	Total Population	23.8	0.2	item-specific RPP	18.6	0.4	*	5.2	0.4
Renter	Total Population	32	0.2	item-specific RPP	58.6	0.6	*	-26.6	0.5
Owner with mortgage	MRI	22.4	0.5	overall RPP	22	0.5	*	0.4	0.2
Owner no mortgage	MRI	19.3	0.5	overall RPP	19.7	0.4	*	-0.3	0.1
Renter	MRI	58.3	0.6	overall RPP	58.3	0.6		-0.1	0.2
Owner with mortgage	MRI	22.4	0.5	item-specific RPP	22.8	0.5	*	-0.4	0.2
Owner no mortgage	MRI	19.3	0.5	item-specific RPP	18.6	0.4	*	0.8	0.1
Renter	MRI	58.3	0.6	item-specific RPP	58.6	0.6	*	-0.3	0.2

* Difference is statistically significant at the 90 percent confidence level.

Source: 2012 Current Population Survey Annual Social and Economic Supplement.

Table 3. Comparing State Level Poverty Rates Using Alternative Indexes to SPM Poverty Rates with No Geographic Adjustment

| | NO GEO | | MRI | | Overall RPP | | Item-Specific RPP | | Change from No Geographic Adjustment | | | | | | |
| | | | | | | | | | No GEO minus MRI | | No GEO minus Overall RPP | | Largest Adjustment | No GEO minus Item-Specific RPP | | Largest Adjustment |
	Estimate	SE	Estimate	SE	Estimate	SE	Estimate	SE	Estimate	SE	Estimate	SE		Estimate	SE	
AL	18.5	1.2	14.5	1.0	14.3	1.0	* 12.6	0.8	* 4.1	0.4	* 4.3	0.5		* 5.9	0.7	RPP
AK	10.8	0.8	12.5	0.9	12.1	0.8	* 15.0	1.0	* -1.7	0.3	* -1.4	0.2		* -4.3	0.5	RPP
AZ	19.9	1.5	19.7	1.5	19.7	1.5	19.6	1.5	0.3	0.3	0.3	0.3		0.3	0.4	
AR	20.5	1.7	15.5	1.3	15.4	1.4	* 13.8	1.2	* 5.1	0.6	* 5.1	0.6		* 6.7	0.8	
CA	16.8	0.4	23.5	0.4	21.0	0.4	* 26.9	0.5	* -6.7	0.2	* -4.2	0.2	MRI	* -10.0	0.3	RPP
CO	14.0	0.7	14.3	0.7	14.5	0.7	15.3	0.8	* -0.2	0.2	* -0.5	0.1		* -1.3	0.3	RPP
CT	9.0	0.5	11.9	0.6	11.4	0.6	12.1	0.6	* -2.8	0.3	* -2.4	0.3		* -3.1	0.3	
DE	12.6	0.7	13.8	0.7	13.2	0.7	13.6	0.8	* -1.1	0.2	* -0.5	0.3		* -0.9	0.4	
DC	16.2	0.8	23.2	0.9	23.0	1.0	27.6	1.0	* -7.0	0.5	* -6.8	0.5		* -11.4	0.7	RPP
FL	17.3	0.5	19.4	0.6	17.6	0.5	19.3	0.6	* -2.1	0.2	* -0.3	0.1	MRI	* -2.0	0.2	
GA	20.4	0.9	18.9	0.9	17.9	0.9	17.3	0.9	* 1.5	0.4	* 2.4	0.3	RPP	* 3.1	0.5	RPP
HI	9.9	0.6	17.3	1.1	15.0	0.9	21.4	1.1	* -7.4	0.7	* -5.1	0.5	MRI	* -11.5	0.7	RPP
ID	15.0	1.3	11.8	1.1	13.2	1.1	12.1	1.1	* 3.2	0.5	* 1.8	0.3	MRI	* 2.9	0.5	
IL	14.8	0.6	15.0	0.6	15.2	0.6	16.2	0.6	* -0.2	0.2	* -0.4	0.3		* -1.4	0.3	RPP
IN	16.5	1.0	14.4	0.8	14.0	0.8	13.5	0.8	* 2.0	0.4	* 2.4	0.5		* 2.9	0.5	
IA	11.1	0.5	8.3	0.5	8.4	0.5	7.7	0.5	* 2.8	0.4	* 2.7	0.4		* 3.4	0.4	
KS	13.3	1.1	11.0	1.1	10.7	1.0	9.8	1.0	* 2.3	0.3	* 2.6	0.3		* 3.5	0.4	RPP
KY	17.9	1.2	13.2	1.0	13.5	0.9	12.1	0.9	* 4.7	0.4	* 4.3	0.5		* 5.8	0.5	RPP
LA	19.8	0.9	16.8	0.9	16.4	0.8	15.8	0.9	* 3.0	0.4	* 3.4	0.3		* 4.1	0.5	
ME	11.9	0.8	10.8	0.7	11.3	0.7	11.0	0.7	* 1.2	0.2	* 0.6	0.2	MRI	* 1.0	0.2	
MD	10.4	0.6	13.5	0.7	12.8	0.6	14.6	0.7	* -3.0	0.3	* -2.4	0.3		* -4.1	0.4	RPP
MA	10.6	0.6	13.6	0.7	12.4	0.7	13.7	0.7	* -3.0	0.3	* -1.8	0.3	MRI	* -3.1	0.3	
MI	14.8	0.7	13.5	0.7	13.3	0.7	12.7	0.7	* 1.3	0.2	* 1.5	0.2		* 2.1	0.2	RPP
MN	10.5	0.7	10.2	0.6	10.0	0.6	10.3	0.6	0.3	0.2	* 0.6	0.3		0.3	0.2	
MS	20.4	1.1	15.6	0.9	14.6	0.9	13.4	0.9	* 4.8	0.8	* 5.7	0.9		* 7.0	1.0	RPP
MO	15.3	1.4	12.8	1.2	12.1	1.2	11.5	1.1	* 2.5	0.3	* 3.2	0.4		* 3.8	0.5	RPP
MT	15.3	1.2	11.9	1.1	13.2	1.1	12.1	1.1	* 3.5	0.5	* 2.1	0.4	MRI	* 3.3	0.5	
NE	11.9	0.7	9.6	0.7	9.3	0.7	8.8	0.7	* 2.4	0.3	* 2.6	0.3		* 3.1	0.4	
NV	16.3	0.8	19.3	1.0	16.6	0.9	18.8	1.0	* -3.0	0.4	* -0.4	0.1	MRI	* -2.5	0.3	
NH	8.5	0.5	10.4	0.6	9.7	0.5	10.9	0.6	* -1.9	0.2	* -1.1	0.2	MRI	* -2.4	0.3	
NJ	11.4	0.7	14.4	0.8	15.6	0.8	18.1	0.9	* -3.0	0.3	* -4.2	0.4	RPP	* -6.7	0.5	RPP
NM	18.1	1.1	15.2	0.9	16.3	1.0	15.4	1.0	* 2.9	0.4	* 1.9	0.4	MRI	* 2.7	0.5	
NY	15.1	0.5	17.7	0.5	19.1	0.5	21.7	0.6	* -2.6	0.2	* -4.0	0.2	RPP	* -6.6	0.4	RPP
NC	16.8	0.9	13.7	0.8	13.4	0.8	12.6	0.7	* 3.1	0.4	* 3.4	0.4		* 4.2	0.5	RPP
ND	12.0	0.9	8.9	0.7	9.3	0.6	9.0	0.7	* 3.1	0.4	* 2.7	0.5		* 3.1	0.4	
OH	15.0	0.7	12.5	0.6	11.7	0.5	11.5	0.6	* 2.5	0.3	* 3.3	0.3	RPP	* 3.5	0.3	RPP
OK	15.3	1.0	12.6	0.8	12.6	0.8	11.2	0.8	* 2.7	0.3	* 2.7	0.4		* 4.1	0.5	RPP
OR	15.6	1.0	14.1	1.0	14.6	1.0	15.1	1.0	* 1.5	0.3	* 1.1	0.3		0.5	0.3	MRI
PA	12.3	0.5	11.4	0.5	12.1	0.5	11.7	0.5	* 0.9	0.2	0.2	0.2	MRI	* 0.6	0.2	
RI	11.8	0.5	12.8	0.6	12.0	0.5	12.7	0.6	* -1.0	0.2	* -0.3	0.1	MRI	* -1.0	0.2	
SC	17.5	0.8	15.1	0.7	14.8	0.7	13.9	0.7	* 2.4	0.4	* 2.7	0.4		* 3.6	0.5	RPP
SD	14.3	1.3	10.9	1.0	10.9	1.0	10.1	0.9	* 3.4	0.5	* 3.5	0.6		* 4.2	0.6	
TN	18.1	1.3	14.7	1.1	14.5	1.1	13.6	1.1	* 3.4	0.4	* 3.6	0.4		* 4.5	0.6	
TX	17.2	0.5	16.3	0.5	16.0	0.5	15.6	0.5	* 0.9	0.2	* 1.3	0.2		* 1.7	0.2	RPP
UT	11.9	1.0	10.5	0.9	11.4	1.0	11.4	1.0	* 1.4	0.2	* 0.5	0.1	MRI	* 0.6	0.1	MRI
VT	8.9	0.7	9.2	0.7	8.9	0.7	10.0	0.8	-0.3	0.3	0.1	0.1		* -1.0	0.3	RPP
VA	12.1	0.7	12.7	0.7	12.4	0.7	13.4	0.7	* -0.6	0.3	-0.3	0.2		* -1.3	0.4	
WA	11.7	0.7	12.0	0.8	12.2	0.7	13.5	0.8	-0.3	0.3	* -0.5	0.2		* -1.8	0.3	RPP
WV	16.2	0.8	12.3	0.7	12.6	0.7	11.0	0.7	* 3.9	0.4	* 3.6	0.4		* 5.2	0.4	RPP
WI	11.8	0.8	10.5	0.8	10.1	0.7	10.2	0.7	* 1.3	0.2	* 1.7	0.2		* 1.6	0.2	
WY	10.9	0.8	9.1	0.7	10.2	0.8	10.0	0.8	* 1.9	0.3	* 0.7	0.1	MRI	* 0.9	0.1	MRI

* Difference is statistically significant at the 90 percent confidence level.

Source: 2010-2012 Current Population Survey Annual Social and Economic Supplements.

Table 4. Comparing Alternative SPM Poverty Rates for States: 2009-2011

State	MRI Index	SE	Overall RPP	SE	Difference MRI minus Overall RPP	SE	Item Specific RPP	SE	Difference MRI minus Item-Spec RPP	SE
AL	14.5	1.0	14.3	1.0	0.2	0.2	12.6	0.8	* 1.8	0.4
AK	12.5	0.9	12.1	0.8	* 0.4	0.1	15.0	1.0	* -2.6	0.4
AZ	19.7	1.5	19.7	1.5	0.0	0.0	19.6	1.5	0.1	0.2
AR	15.5	1.3	15.4	1.4	0.1	0.2	13.8	1.2	* 1.6	0.3
CA	23.5	0.4	21.0	0.4	* 2.5	0.1	26.9	0.5	* -3.4	0.2
CO	14.3	0.7	14.5	0.7	* -0.3	0.1	15.3	0.8	* -1.0	0.2
CT	11.9	0.6	11.4	0.6	* 0.4	0.2	12.1	0.6	* -0.3	0.1
DE	13.8	0.7	13.2	0.7	* 0.6	0.2	13.6	0.8	0.2	0.3
DC	23.2	0.9	23.0	1.0	0.2	0.3	27.6	1.0	* -4.4	0.4
FL	19.4	0.6	17.6	0.5	* 1.8	0.2	19.3	0.6	0.1	0.1
GA	18.9	0.9	17.9	0.9	* 0.9	0.2	17.3	0.9	* 1.6	0.2
HI	17.3	1.1	15.0	0.9	* 2.3	0.4	21.4	1.1	* -4.1	0.5
ID	11.8	1.1	13.2	1.1	* -1.4	0.3	12.1	1.1	* -0.3	0.1
IL	15.0	0.6	15.2	0.6	* -0.2	0.1	16.2	0.6	* -1.2	0.2
IN	14.4	0.8	14.0	0.8	* 0.4	0.2	13.5	0.8	* 0.9	0.3
IA	8.3	0.5	8.4	0.5	-0.1	0.1	7.7	0.5	* 0.6	0.1
KS	11.0	1.1	10.7	1.0	* 0.4	0.1	9.8	1.0	* 1.2	0.2
KY	13.2	1.0	13.5	0.9	* -0.4	0.2	12.1	0.9	* 1.1	0.2
LA	16.8	0.9	16.4	0.8	* 0.4	0.2	15.8	0.9	* 1.0	0.2
ME	10.8	0.7	11.3	0.7	* -0.5	0.2	11.0	0.7	* -0.2	0.1
MD	13.5	0.7	12.8	0.6	* 0.6	0.2	14.6	0.7	* -1.1	0.2
MA	13.6	0.7	12.4	0.7	* 1.2	0.3	13.7	0.7	-0.2	0.1
MI	13.5	0.7	13.3	0.7	* 0.1	0.1	12.7	0.7	* 0.8	0.1
MN	10.2	0.6	10.0	0.6	* 0.2	0.1	10.3	0.6	-0.1	0.1
MS	15.6	0.9	14.6	0.9	* 1.0	0.2	13.4	0.9	* 2.2	0.4
MO	12.8	1.2	12.1	1.2	* 0.7	0.2	11.5	1.1	* 1.3	0.2
MT	11.9	1.1	13.2	1.1	* -1.4	0.2	12.1	1.1	-0.2	0.1
NE	9.6	0.7	9.3	0.7	* 0.3	0.1	8.8	0.7	* 0.8	0.2
NV	19.3	1.0	16.6	0.9	* 2.6	0.4	18.8	1.0	* 0.5	0.1
NH	10.4	0.6	9.7	0.5	* 0.7	0.2	10.9	0.6	* -0.6	0.1
NJ	14.4	0.8	15.6	0.8	* -1.2	0.2	18.1	0.9	* -3.7	0.4
NM	15.2	0.9	16.3	1.0	* -1.1	0.2	15.4	1.0	-0.2	0.2
NY	17.7	0.5	19.1	0.5	* -1.3	0.1	21.7	0.6	* -3.9	0.2
NC	13.7	0.8	13.4	0.8	* 0.3	0.1	12.6	0.7	* 1.1	0.2
ND	8.9	0.7	9.3	0.6	* -0.4	0.2	9.0	0.7	0.0	0.1
OH	12.5	0.6	11.7	0.5	* 0.8	0.1	11.5	0.6	* 1.0	0.1
OK	12.6	0.8	12.6	0.8	0.1	0.1	11.2	0.8	* 1.4	0.3

Table 4. Comparing Alternative SPM Poverty Rates for States: 2009-2011

State	MRI Index	SE	Overall RPP	SE	Difference MRI minus Overall RPP	SE	Item Specific RPP	SE	Difference MRI minus Item-Spec RPP	SE
OR	14.1	1.0	14.6	1.0	* -0.5	0.1	15.1	1.0	* -1.1	0.2
PA	11.4	0.5	12.1	0.5	* -0.7	0.1	11.7	0.5	* -0.3	0.1
RI	12.8	0.6	12.0	0.5	* 0.8	0.1	12.7	0.6	0.1	0.1
SC	15.1	0.7	14.8	0.7	* 0.3	0.1	13.9	0.7	* 1.2	0.2
SD	10.9	1.0	10.9	1.0	0.1	0.1	10.1	0.9	* 0.8	0.1
TN	14.7	1.1	14.5	1.1	0.2	0.1	13.6	1.1	* 1.1	0.2
TX	16.3	0.5	16.0	0.5	* 0.4	0.1	15.6	0.5	* 0.8	0.1
UT	10.5	0.9	11.4	1.0	* -0.8	0.2	11.4	1.0	* -0.8	0.2
VT	9.2	0.7	8.9	0.7	0.3	0.2	10.0	0.8	* -0.8	0.2
VA	12.7	0.7	12.4	0.7	* 0.3	0.1	13.4	0.7	* -0.8	0.2
WA	12.0	0.8	12.2	0.7	-0.2	0.2	13.5	0.8	* -1.5	0.2
WV	12.3	0.7	12.6	0.7	* -0.3	0.1	11.0	0.7	* 1.3	0.2
WI	10.5	0.8	10.1	0.7	* 0.4	0.1	10.2	0.7	* 0.3	0.1
WY	9.1	0.7	10.2	0.8	* -1.2	0.3	10.0	0.8	* -1.0	0.2

* Difference is statistically significant at the 90 percent confidence level.

Source: 2010-2012 Current Population Survey Annual Social and Economic Supplements.